The *Mike Douglas* Cookbook

The *Mike Douglas* COOKBOOK

by *Mike Douglas*

with *Dan Morris*

Funk & Wagnalls

NEW YORK

This book is dedicated to the many people who made it possible:
to all those who watch my show on television every day; to those who
appear on it; to those who cook on it; to those whose recipes appear in
these pages . . . and especially to my wife and to my mother,
not only for their recipes but also for their love

Contents

Preface

When I was approached about writing a cookbook with Mike Douglas I was quite happy that I had been chosen because I knew the monetary rewards would be good and no writer, not even a cookbook writer, can live by bread alone.

But still I had doubts about saying yes because I know about the many show business people who decide they'd like to write a book and then contract with a ghost writer to write it for them. And, though some of my best friends are ghosts, I am not about to be one myself. At least not upon this earth.

So I said there would have to be equal billing and, much to my surprise, I was told that Mike wouldn't have it any other way, that he does not believe in ghosts either. The by-line would read "By Mike Douglas and Dan Morris."

We made a date for the two of us to meet and go to work a couple of days later. Meanwhile I'd read up on all that the press had to say about him. About the clean-cut wholesome American boy who didn't smoke, didn't drink, loved his wife, loved his kids. I laughed a cynic's laugh and thought they're all alike, they all get to believe what their claques say about them.

Then I met Mike, started to work with him, and I discovered that all those published biographies were not filled with press agentry. They were filled with fact. Mike doesn't smoke, he doesn't drink, he does love his wife, the only one he ever had, and the sun rises and sets on his kids.

Not only that, but I also discovered that Mike does not need anyone to write a book either for him or with him. He's as articulate as anyone I've ever met. He has a way with words. His spoken words are good enough to be written words. But he does not have the time to write a book.

The Mike Douglas Show is televised for an hour and a half a day, but Mike puts in eight or ten additional hours a day programming, planning, researching, rehearsing, doing a hundred and one behind-the-scenes things. Add seven hours a day to that for sleeping, a few hours more for eating, shaving, bathing, dressing, and commuting to and from work and there isn't any time left to write a book. Especially not when he has to work in the time to appear as a guest on someone else's television show, to cut a record, to make a movie or to emcee a Thanksgiving Day or Rose Bowl parade.

That's why, I soon discovered, Mike's people asked me to write this book with him instead of letting him write it himself as he wanted to. But, as I said, I did not know that until I worked with Mike for a while.

The way we worked was simple. We'd sit down with a tape recorder between us and I'd ask questions and Mike would give the answers. Then I'd take the tapes home with me, I thought at first, to put into readable English. But, listening to them, I discovered that Mike's words needed no rewriting. He speaks for publication the way he sounds on the air. Free, easy, breezy.

For me to do anything more than to change the sequence here and there or to add punctuation or to see to the testing of the recipes and to break in with an occasional question or parenthetical aside would be unfair both to Mike and to you, the readers, who in all likelihood are part of his daily television audience and wouldn't have him any other way.

Therefore I couldn't in good conscience still share a joint by-line with Mike Douglas because I had to be as fair with him as he was with me. So, instead, the credit lines now read "By Mike Douglas with Dan Morris." I shell the peas and cross the T's.

Which, incidentally, gives me leeway to say parenthetical things about Mike that he couldn't, shouldn't and wouldn't say for himself because, just as all those press clippings said, Mike Douglas *is* a nice guy.

Dan Morris

I

You Asked for It

1

But Kelly Loves It!

Almost the first question asked of me when Dan and I first sat down to work on this book was:

Mike, why do you want to write a cookbook?

I replied that I didn't but that *you* did. By you I mean the people who are good enough to watch me and my guests every day on television. As you know, the co-host every week prepares one of his or her favorite recipes on the air. Some are good, some are not, some are out of this world, some are laughable and others might put a gourmet, whatever that is, to shame.

But, good or bad, we then send copies of the recipe-of-the-week to everyone who asks for it. The fewest so far has been thirty thousand, I won't say for whose recipe, and the highest has been seventy thousand for a very down-to-earth way of cooking hot dogs and chili con carne.

And every week, scattered among those thirty thousand to seventy thousand requests for recipes are a few thousand asking us to put them all together in one cookbook.

We have picked out about one hundred and fifty recipes that we think everyone would be happy to add to his collection and those are the ones that you'll find in this book, together with some from my mother, some from my wife and some from guests on the show who, for one reason or another, couldn't get around to preparing them on the air.

I didn't think much about food until the show caught on and

letters started arriving from all over the country. *The Mike Douglas Show* began in Cleveland on just one station. The mail then, naturally, was a trickle and of course none of it ever came from farther than fifty or a hundred miles away.

We had a cooking segment at least once a week and even then the letters that we received were mainly about food. I'd say the requests for recipes ran two to one over all the other mail we received.

And now it's at least five to one!

No matter what else happens on the show during the week, no matter how much of a storm we may whip up, no matter how controversial a guest may be, no matter how badly, occasionally, we goof, the week's mail for everything else combined has leveled off to between six thousand and seven thousand letters. But we have just one guest recipe a week and the requests for that one recipe run anywhere from thirty to seventy thousand!

We discovered on *The Mike Douglas Show* what I guess everybody else in the world already knew—that people like to eat!! And most of them are always on the lookout for something new, not way-out dishes which only one out of a thousand people ever eat, but mainly new ways of cooking the old standbys. Or the inexpensive. Steak, eggs, chops, hamburgers, frankfurters, things like that.

That I know is true in my family. We're basically meat and potato eaters but we're always willing to try a new way of cooking them. That's why we have so many cookbooks in our house, and that's why I know that the thousands of you who have asked for this cookbook are serious about it.

I'm quite sure you want it only because it will contain recipes that you would want to prepare in your homes for your families. You don't want them only because they looked good to you at the time you saw them on television. I'm quite sure you don't want these recipes simply because some celebrity or other prepares them that way. I'm quite sure your husband would have harsh things to say about it if that were your only criterion for putting what you did on his dinner plate.

BUT KELLY LOVES IT!

In other words, I'm quite sure you'd want—and like—the recipes in this book even if it were called *The Mike Dowd Cookbook* instead of *The Mike Douglas Cookbook.*

It could be called *The Mike Dowd Cookbook,* you know, because that's my name, although you all know me as Mike Douglas. Douglas is a good show business name. Everyone can pronounce it. Everyone can spell it. No one is likely to confuse it with someone else's name.

So I'm known on television as Mike Douglas.

But I vote and I drive a car and I live as Mike Dowd. My daughters are carried on school rolls as Dowd, not Douglas. My wife is Mrs. Michael Delaney Dowd, Jr., not Mrs. Mike Douglas.

Let me tell you about my family. There's my wife, Genevieve, our identical twin daughters, Michele and Christine, who at this writing are twenty-three, and then there is the light of all our lives, our youngest daughter, Kelly Anne, aged ten.

The show was still coming out of Cleveland and so we were still living in Ohio when the twins finished high school and went on to college. Christine was a student at Ohio State when she met her future husband, who then was a student at Ohio University. She finished her freshman year and they were married that summer. Mr. and Mrs. Paul Voinovich, a Serbian name. They have two lovely little daughters, Deborah Lynn and Cynthia Ann.

By the time this book is published Paul should be a practicing architect in Cleveland, probably working alongside his father, who is quite a prominent architect there. Paul is a hard-working boy, a real hustler in every good sense of the word. He's not afraid to work. He faces up to responsibility. When Debbie was born he left Ohio U. and started going to the Case Institute of Technology nights so he could work days and support his family.

We're proud of Paul and happy for Christine. He's a wonderful husband, a wonderful father.

Michele was graduated from the University of Toledo in 1968 and didn't waste a minute becoming a first grade teacher there, she's that crazy about kids and teaching. She'll be a fine teacher.

Kelly Anne is in the fifth grade at Sacred Heart Academy here in Philadelphia and you might say she is ten going on sixteen, I think because of having sisters thirteen years older. She is almost precocious, but very sweet and dear with a very sensitive face. She's petite, the smallest in her class, and has big blue eyes and dimples, and sandy-colored hair. Very Irish-looking, with a few freckles sprinkled across the bridge of her nose. The name Kelly truly fits her.

She is really a bright child. We weren't aware of how bright until she changed schools recently and they gave her an IQ test. She was only eight at the time but the tests showed she had the intelligence of an eleven-year-old. We were very pleased.

I don't know how this is going to fit into a cookbook, but Kelly doesn't have much of an appetite. She eats just about enough to keep a sparrow going. When she eats, which we think is rarely, she loves baked potato with lots of butter and ham and she could literally live on hamburgers. Happily, though, she drinks—for her —lots of milk and eats lots of salad so she's rosy cheeked and healthy and full of energy.

One Halloween I came home early to pack a bag. She came home from school, raced up the stairs to her room to change into her costume, spotted me and shouted, "What are you going to be, Dad?"

I, proud as can be, said I had to catch a plane to Chicago where I was going to be honored as Broadcasting's Man of the Year.

And our little girl, God bless her, shouted back, "That's nice, I'm going to be Raggedy Ann!"

That's my Kelly Anne.

All of our girls have sandy hair and a few freckles and all of us in the family have blue eyes, but Michele and Christine look more like me, while Kelly is the one who really looks like her mother.

Mike, what does your wife look like?

When I married her she had brown hair but it's blonde now to hide a couple of strands of gray. It's very lovely, though. It tends to soften her face. Genevieve is a very beautiful woman and I don't say so because she is my wife. Everyone is in complete accord on this. She's beautiful and, I might add, also beautiful within. A wonderful wife, a wonderful mother.

How did you meet her?

We met when I was working on my first professional job as staff soloist at WKY Radio in Oklahoma City. I was nineteen, alone in a strange town and a long way from home. Her brother was the continuity man at the station and he felt sorry for me so he invited me out to their home for Christmas dinner.

That's when I met Genevieve. She was sixteen and we were married when she was seventeen. In fact I proposed on her seventeenth birthday, yet for most of the year in between we never actually went out together because of her age. I felt she was too young to go with boys.

But she was all I could ever think of. I couldn't get her out of my mind. One night she came to the radio station with another boy. We were playing transcriptions when he walked out of the room to get another armful of records and that's when I first got up nerve enough to ask her if she would go out with me sometime. That's how the whole thing started.

Our love is one of those things. The first time we saw each other, that was it. From the first moment at that Christmas dinner.

Mike, this is a cookbook. Do you remember what you had for dinner?

I don't remember anything but her. I can't even tell you whether it was turkey, or duck or goose or what. People talk about love at first sight. Her name was Genevieve and she had brown hair and blue eyes and there wasn't anything else on my mind from that first moment on.

We were married before she finished her senior year at high school. But she did graduate when I went off for my Navy stint in 1943. She should have gone to college really but I never gave her the chance. I wanted her with me and she wanted to be with me.

When I went to the University of Wisconsin for the Navy's V-12 Program, she went up to Madison with me and stayed with me all the while I was in school.

Is she a good cook?

Oh, she's a wonderful cook. She's marvelous. She's just a marvelous woman. She's a great mother. I haven't noticed that she's changed her ways a bit because of our good fortune. She has kept both feet, and mine, too, on the ground and she is just as marvelous a wife as she ever was. We still find ourselves doing the things we used to do and always did even though our lives have changed a great deal and we can afford much more.

What kind of things?

Oh, like we go for walks and hold hands when we walk down the street. This kind of thing, corny as it might sound. Especially when we're away from the children, maybe in New York City or wherever we are because of some professional engagement and Kelly can't be with us because of school. Gen goes with me and we do all those corny things that are so wonderful. And it's not because we're trying to impress anyone, it's just because this is the way it's always been, this is what we've always done.

Then why did you change your name?

Oh no, we never legalized the change. We're still Mr. and Mrs. Michael Delaney Dowd, Jr. Mike Douglas is simply a name that Kay Kyser gave me when I joined him in 1945. One of his closest friends was Michael Todd and Kay didn't want any confusion, especially since names are so easily misunderstood on radio. People would send me mail—D-o-d-d, D-a-u-d, D-o-w-e—everything but D-o-w-d.

Kay Kyser was right. Mike Dowd was not a good radio name. So I became Mike Douglas but, as I said, only professionally.

Your daily routine, Mike. What's that like?

I don't think there's enough room in the book to tell it all, but let's begin. I get up with Gen and Kelly at about a quarter to seven every morning and while Gen's scurrying to get Kelly all set for school I shower and shave. I try to move faster but I usually get down to breakfast when they're just about finishing, so I sit there all alone reading my paper.

Who cooks the breakfast?

Why, Gen does of course. We have help but the cook doesn't

take over until about ten o'clock and I prefer it that way because I want that first meal in the morning to taste like my wife's cooking. I eat a very hearty breakfast because I'm not able to have lunch until about three o'clock in the afternoon and it takes quite a bit of fuel to keep me going through the show.

The show is seen at a great variety of times on the 190 or so stations that carry it, but we actually tape it between twelve-thirty and two o'clock every day, just the time that anyone else would be knocking off for lunch.

What do you eat for breakfast?

I have eggs done in a special way that Gen has (see recipe on page 63) with some nice crisp bacon, a large glass of orange juice, sometimes a cup of black coffee and always whole wheat toast with honey. Honey is a great pick-me-up, a great energy builder. Sometimes before the show, while getting things in order in the studio, I have a cup of tea with honey in it instead of sugar.

I'm a great one for protein, as you know. My lunch is the same thing every day because it really stokes me up, sees me through the next few hours of preliminary preparation for the next day's show.

(D.M. notes: I knew because I'd had lunch with Mike twice up to that time, both times at the same place, and both times the same thing for both of us because, this being Mike's home base, he did the ordering. The place was Arthur's, a fine restaurant just a block or so up Philadelphia's Walnut Street from Westinghouse's KYW television studios, which have been home for The Mike Douglas Show *since 1965.*

At Arthur's every day Mike eats what has come to be known there as The Mike Douglas Lunch:

6 oz. tenderloin steak, ¾ inch thick and broiled medium-rare

3 slices beefsteak tomatoes, each about 1 inch thick and sprinkled with about 3 oz. bleu or Roquefort cheese, broken into about ½-inch pieces and topped with wine vinegar and olive oil to taste

1 pumpernickel salt stick

1 cup black coffee, unsweetened

Steak, of course, is normal fare anywhere but the tomato-and-bleu cheese combination is by no means usual. So the next time I was at Arthur's with Mike I asked Herman Kahn, the proprietor, where he'd hit upon it and he replied, "I didn't. Mike did. The first time he ever came in here he asked for it and he's been eating it almost every day since. How long is it now, Mike, two years, three years?"

"A long time," said Mike, "but it seems like yesterday."

"Yes," said Herman, "and we'd like to put three anchovy fillets, just three little anchovies, on the plate with the tomatoes and cheese but he won't let us." Herman looked and sounded hurt, so I let him put them on mine and I'm glad that I did. But then I wrote a seafood cookbook once, while Mike did not, so maybe I'm prejudiced in favor of fish.)

Back now to Mike . . .

I seldom eat bread although I can't resist those pumpernickel salt sticks at Arthur's. Except for that one at lunch and my morning whole wheat toast and honey, I never eat bread with a meal. In the evening, we always have our meat and our vegetables. I stay with the proteins and mainly the yellow vegetables. The proteins for energy, the yellow vegetables because I like them, although I know they're good for me, too. My favorite is squash.

Do you have any favorite recipes that you'd want included in the book?

I just might have or rather Gen just might have. My cooking is mainly confined to the outdoor charcoal grill and to hamburgers, steaks and chops. Along with potatoes and corn wrapped in foil.

What's your favorite food, Mike?

Outside of the things I just mentioned—charcoal-broiled steaks and chops and salads of course—I'm a great dessert man. That, I guess, is because I don't drink and I've got to get that sugar someplace.

What's your favorite dessert?

I'm a great cake man. I can't eat too much of it, though, because of instant jowl, you know, getting fat in all the wrong places. But I love devil's food cake. The kind with the white icing. That's my favorite cake. And I like pie, warm apple pie in a bowl with milk. And Gen makes an applesauce nut bread (see recipe on page 151) that's a perfect snack before going to bed.

What's a typical evening meal, dinner, at your house?

We like a fresh fruit cocktail, never the canned stuff, or a cup of onion soup to get things started, then lamb chops or a roast or occasionally a well-done pork chop along with two vegetables and a salad. The dessert usually comes a couple of hours later. The cooks prepares all this, mainly because Gen is so busy with all the things that she has to do because she is the wife of Mike Douglas that she just doesn't have the time.

But you can be sure that the food the cook puts before us is prepared in strict accordance with Gen's recipes and instructions. She tells him exactly what we want and that's exactly what he gives us. Sure, he adds a little something to a recipe now and then but only with Gen's approval. She does all the planning.

She even does all the food shopping, checks the ads every week, finds out what the best buys are, what's in season and what is not, and then takes off for the supermarket. I marvel at her for it because I imagine it's quite unusual nowadays to see a woman who can afford to be doing other things pushing a cart up and down the aisles, checking prices, checking labels, checking weights, trying to figure out unsuccessfully like housewives everywhere if king size is a better value than family size.

You'd think that women who can afford live-in help would leave it all up to them. But not my wife. Not my Gen. She wants to know what's being put on that table.

Does Kelly go food shopping with her?

Oh yes. Kelly goes everywhere with her. And me. Kelly is our sunshine. She's our little caboose. She's everything to us. Where we go, she goes. What we do, she does.

Does Kelly do any cooking?

If you can call putting practically a quarter-pound of butter on a baked potato cooking then you might say that Kelly cooks! Otherwise no.

You said she is a great salad eater. What's her favorite?

The salad that *I* make. Caesar salad. Oh yes, I'm the Caesar salad maker in our house. Kelly loves it; we all love it.

What's your recipe?

Well, it's a recipe that I've kept adding to or taking away from throughout the years. A little more of this. A little less of that. Just a lot of experimenting, changing, improvising. It started out with a basic Caesar salad recipe that I found somewhere, I don't remember where, and now it has grown into a "Caesar Douglas" salad.

But what exactly is the recipe now?

Well, I start out with the wooden bowl and rub the garlic on the bowl and then the usual, you know, the egg, the coddled egg, the anchovies of which as you know I'm not otherwise too overly fond but you need them in a Caesar salad. Then come the usual seasonings, you know, a pinch of this, a pinch of that or sometimes a pinch of this instead of that. I like my Caesar salad with romaine lettuce. I throw in a few things here and there like a little dry mustard and certain types of vinegars—we'd better get Gen to check the labels to see exactly what kind. It's really a favorite of ours and as I said, Kelly loves it!

(I said, Mike it certainly sounds like a recipe that's decidedly and distinctively different but I'm afraid that as it stands right now it will be difficult to include in the book. After all, I said, recipes have to stand still long enough to be written down before they can be published. So Mike promised to measure everything and to write it all down the next time he made a Caesar Douglas salad. He was true to his word and you'll find the recipe on page 53, in close proximity to Casear salad recipes à la Shelley Winters and Michael O'Shea. We can't promise though that what was Mike's recipe then will necessarily be his recipe now. But it's a safe bet that Kelly will love it because her father, Michael Delaney Dowd, Jr., made it. D.M.)

2

From Legion Hall to A House on the Main Line

I've had traumatic experiences only twice in my life and neither one of them had anything to do with making a Caesar salad.

One of them was walking down the aisle with my daughter Christine when she married. After telling my wife "Gee, don't cry, let's get through this without tears," I broke down both at the rehearsal and at the ceremony.

And when I saw my daughter Michele graduated from college, I cried. I can't explain why. I guess that's a very proud moment in a father's life. *My* daughter, *my* Michele, graduating trom college. Now she's teaching in the Toledo public schools system and at the same time working for her Master's in education. She loves teaching and it's so important that we have good teachers. I'm so proud of her I can't explain the feeling.

It's worth living to have things like that happen to you and to members of your family. They give me, I guess they give every father, things to look back upon. Memories. I've got my full share of them and I wouldn't change a single one.

Now I can laugh at many of them even though at the time they happened they were far from laughing matters. It's not easy, traveling around the country keeping hotel and club dates, living from one hotel room to another. And everywhere I went, Gen was right at my side, she carrying one of the twins, me carrying the other. Our cooking on hot plates kept many a house detective busy trying to tell what room the smells were coming from.

THE MIKE DOUGLAS COOKBOOK

That's what it used to be like. But it isn't any more, thanks to Genevieve. She kept me hanging in there, and I think that if ever I had to say in one word how she did it, I'd say love. We have love in all its fullest meaning in our family, in our house.

It's always been that way. From the day I was born, I'd say. We never had much in the way of material things when I was a boy, but we had each other. We were a family, never owning a home, moving from one place and then to another, but always having each other.

Dad was a general freight agent for the Canadian Pacific Railroad in Chicago. Mother was more than just a housewife. I grew up in the middle of the Depression and Mother had to do more than just take care of a house. She had to figure out ways of bringing in extra pennies from here and there to make sure there was always the right kind of food to put on the table.

She was, she is, quite a cook. She had to be and I guess that one of the reasons why I decided to write a cookbook was so that I could include many of her recipes in it. I have a brother and a sister, both older than me, and when we sat down to eat one of Mom's meals we never left anything on our plates. Not because it would be wasteful, but because everything she made tasted so good. I can recommend every recipe in this book (if not, they wouldn't have been included), but none more so than those that come from Mother Dowd's kitchen.

Mike, how did you get into show business?

That's a good question. My brother is in the roofing and tiling business. My sister is a housewife with five children. My father thought it was mighty strange, to say the least, for me to want to do what I'm doing. So how did I get into show business? It certainly didn't run in the family. I didn't follow in anyone's footsteps and no one is following in mine.

Mother tells me that I actually sang before I talked, that she would put me to sleep with Fritz Kreisler records and that I would hum melodies long before I could say anything more than ma ma and da da.

So, you see, even as an infant I loved music. I still do and I always have. There was no money for any formal musical training in those Depression days. I did the best that I could, listened to radio constantly, listened to the best singers around, picked up little bits and pieces here and there and when I was about eleven I started to think about it seriously.

I went to the Chicago Theater once with Mother and saw a stage show and a fellow came on wearing cocoa-brown slacks, brown and white shoes and a beautiful white coat that looked as if he had been poured into it. Beautiful clothes and he told jokes and he made people laugh and he looked like he had a million dollars in each pocket. I thought to myself, gee, what a great way to make a living. Stand up in front of people and make them happy, you know, and to have clothes like that and shoes like that. Shoes with complete soles on them, I mean, and I thought, gee, wouldn't that be nice.

It stayed in the back of my mind and then when I finally got into high school, I'd save up my lunch money and when I'd finally have enough I'd cut classes and I'd go down to the Chicago Theater and see the stage shows. Those were the days, vaudeville days, when they had the big names. You name the singer, they sang there, and I saw and heard them all and learned a little something from every one of them.

Times were tough and we all had to pitch in and help. Dad had a good job but it really wasn't enough and so I always had some sort of odd job or another. And that, I think, is very healthy. It should be happening in more households, especially today. Then I don't think we'd be having all of the problems with the juveniles that we're having now.

Kids can still get the kinds of jobs that I got. I had a paper route, I delivered groceries, I worked in a paint store, things like that. Those kinds of after-school jobs are still around and more kids ought to be looking for them. I never knew what it was like to get a full week's pay and put it in my pocket to spend as I pleased. I always went home and gave at least half of it to Mom to help out with the grocery bills and whatever.

That's what I mean by a family working together. I think it

makes a better person out of you and I'm happy that I had to do it. Now that I look back I wouldn't have wanted it any other way and maybe that's what our country needs more of right now. I know that it paid off for me.

My wife and I are from relatively poor families but as far as happiness and love were concerned we were very rich. Both Gen's parents and mine were good people and we received much love as young people and that could be why we're having no problems now.

But getting back to my teenage working days . . .

I think my most memorable paying job was the night I got five dollars for doing a show in the American Legion Hall in Forest Park, Illinois. I emceed the whole show, I did a spot of my own, I introduced the other acts and I got five dollars. I thought it was all the money in the world. I was fifteen or sixteen. I was in high school and I thought gee, isn't that great, I did something that I enjoyed and I got five dollars for it! It's been that way all my life. I think I'm fortunate for many reasons, but I think that I'm especially fortunate in that I'm doing something that I truly love and I'm being paid for it. I think that's important for any human being. I think that's why people come to me from time to time and ask me if I'm ever despondent, if I'm ever unhappy because I look like such a happy person on television.

The truth is that we all have our moments when we're depressed and down, but generally speaking I'm basically a very happy and a very well-adjusted guy, especially for a guy in this business. I don't have any, as they say, hang-ups. I have a wonderful wife, a wonderful family, and luckily I've got both my feet on the ground and I don't have any plans of changing that attitude and that way of life.

You know, I finish my work and I come home and I'm delighted to be here. I'm happy with my home life, I'm happy with my wife and my kids. I'm proud of them.

It's great, Mike, just great, that you're so well adjusted, but we were talking about how you got into show business, how you got to have all this. Remember? (We were seated in Mike's den in his Main Line mansion, sunk deep in full leather chairs, the

walls lined with mementoes, and the mantel over the fireplace, too,
everything from a gold golf trophy to an Emmy to a drawing by
Kelly.)

Sorry, Dan, but I get carried away by all this when I think how
it used to be. The lean years.

When I was in high school I would take summer jobs with
traveling bands around the Chicago area as a male vocalist. One
summer I worked on a C & B Great Lakes cruiser. It was great
experience. I lived aboard all summer, I got thirty-five dollars a
week plus room and board. What a wonderful summer that was,
and I guess that is when I really made up my mind that this was
the life for me.

So here I am, the only member of my family, past or present,
ever to go into show business. Dad, when he heard that I wanted
to sing for a living, thought it was kind of strange. You know, the
old-fashioned outlook: there are a lot of peculiar people in show
business. That's what parents thought in those days.

He didn't realize that somewhere there was an end of the rain-
bow, a pay-off, a great big pot of gold. And this is it.

(There came a rich silence to the room. Mike was far away
in time, alone with his thoughts, thinking, I knew, of the harsh years
between then and now when the most important thing he had going
for him was a wife who matched him hardship for hardship, who
wouldn't let him quit, who rekindled confidence in him by showing
in every word and deed that she had confidence in him. But all
of that is a better subject for another book, not a cookbook. So I
sat quietly, too, letting the warmth of that room, of that house, big
as it was, of that family, soak into me. Then, after a time, Mike
spoke again but even before he spoke I knew that he knew that I
was now wondering how come a guy with such humble beginnings
could now be living in a house such as this . . . thirty-one rooms,
marble halls, mirrored walls, the works. D.M.)

You're about to ask me about all this, *Mike said,* turning his
head practically full circle. Well, it all ties in with hardships, about
being on the road all those years, about living in one room, with
babies, with diapers to wash and no place to wash them, with bottles

to heat and only a hot plate on which to heat them.

With all too often only one hundred or one hundred twenty-five dollars a week coming in and sometimes weeks with nothing at all coming in, not even enough to buy a can of beans except with what Gen had tucked away in the toe of her shoe or some such place.

We went through four or five years of that kind of living and then when we thought we had it good all that we really had was a job that paid maybe two hundred dollars a week. That's why I say I have a very special gal. She never lost faith, she never let me lose faith. There were times when I could see that her nerves were ready to come apart and I'd want to call everything off and I'd want to get a job selling real estate or insurance or something, anything to keep her from falling apart. But she'd pull herself together and she'd pull me back together.

We bought this house to make up for all those long, lean years. We're enjoying the luxury of having more rooms than we know what to do with, having a few acres of land that we haven't yet set foot on.

All we have besides our family and our loved ones is our home. That's why this home means so much to us. Before this the only other home we ever owned was a little GI house in Burbank, California, but about the only time we ever lived in it was when I was out of work because otherwise we were always on the road.

So when *The Mike Douglas Show* became a success, with Philadelphia as its base, Gen and I knew that at last we could settle down with a measure of security that comes only from knowing that you're going to be in one place for some time to come.

Well, then, what kind of house to look for? We used to look through movie magazines and see pictures of a star standing in front of a house like this and so this was something that we always dreamed about. And here we were in Philadelphia, the city around which so many moneyed people long ago carved out their estates and built their mansions, down here in the suburbs along the Pennsylvania Railroad's Main Line. And now so many of those estates are standing vacant with only a "for sale" sign to guard them.

We knew that we were being frivolous, that we were being extravagant, but when we saw this thirty-one-room Tudor house it was a case of love at first sight. But still we were cautious, coming up through hard times the way we had; we didn't run right out and buy it. Instead we consulted Vincent Andrews, our business manager. We took him out to look at the house and we asked him if we could afford it. Yes, he said, you can but do you really want it?

Yes, we said, we do. We really do. We were somewhat sheepish. I know I was like a kid looking longingly at a red wagon and afraid his father would say no, you can't have it. But all Vinny said was, well, go ahead and buy it.

So we bought it.

What we didn't know until a lot later was that Vinny, being a business manager, already had checked out the value of the property and he knew that no matter what happened, dollar for dollar, we couldn't lose.

Truthfully, I was kind of shocked when I first saw the house from the outside. It seemed so ostentatious, so pretentious, I couldn't see myself living in something like that. But then when I got inside the house . . . you know how you feel happiness from the walls of certain homes the moment you walk into them? Well, that's the way I felt. This house, to me, felt so warm inside and so comfortable and this room that we're sitting in, this library, I fell in love with it. I thought, gee, this could be my room, wouldn't it be nice to have a nice easy chair here, a nice reading lamp, lots of books.

(Mike settled deeper into his chair and was still, content purring from every pore. My eyes wandered around the room with its heavy, hand-carved oak coffee table, its gleaming grain showing through the mounds of magazines; floor-to-ceiling shelves jam-packed with books; chairs that were meant for sitting, not showing; lamps that were meant for reading; a fireplace that was meant for winter fires. D.M.)

I didn't know when we moved in, *Mike said,* that this room would have that added feature there on the mantel, that Emmy. It kind of sets the room off. And it sums up the story of my life.

From rags to riches because I got lucky with *The Mike Douglas Show*.

So, all in all, we're very happy that we purchased the house. It's very private up here, it's in a lovely area, it's near a fine school for Kelly, it's everything that we want. Tell the truth, though, happy as we are here, I wouldn't want to end my days in a place like this. What I really want and what someday we'll really have is a little house near a golf course, close enough to drive my golf cart from the eighteenth green, with a carport to park it under and with golfing weather twelve months of the year.

Like I said, it's the show that makes it all possible. Or, more than the show, all the wonderful people who let us know in so many ways that they like to have us in their homes every day. The letters they write, the nice things they say, sometimes they almost make me feel that I'm some sort of a missionary, spreading cheer, bringing so many different kinds of people together for an hour and a half every day. Imagine all those people tuned in to me every day doing something in common with each other though they've never met. Sharing me!

All of us who go to make up *The Mike Douglas Show* (I'm just the guy up front) have hit upon a happy formula for making people happy and we're going to keep it this way: the interviews, the jokes, the horseplay, the songs, the frivolity, the seriousness, the informality.

And you know, I have more fun than anybody. Especially when a guest is trying to cook something, because that's when things go wrong more often than anything else that we do. Like when Gypsy Rose Lee brought not only a very extensive, expensive wardrobe to see her through a week of co-hosting, but also even brought with her her own pots and pans!

When it came time for Gypsy to prepare a recipe, she was ready . . . and, as a result, there was disaster. Gypsy was to demonstrate how to make an omelet that she'd created. I was to be her not-so-able assistant, with only one thing to do. Pick up the frying pan when Gypsy said "turn" and flop it over to transfer it, uncooked side down, to a pan that Gypsy was holding.

But . . . what a scene! The pans that Gypsy brought with her had screw-on handles, Gypsy hadn't screwed mine on tightly enough and so . . . you know the rest. I picked up, I turned, the handle came off and that runny, partially cooked omelet landed all over the stove. Not all of it, just the part that didn't land on Gypsy's beautiful gown! But it's a good omelet. I know because we tried it at home and besides we got tens of thousands of requests for the recipe. You'll find it on page 66.

Everybody on the show gets into the act when it's time to cook. One day Durwood Kirby was showing how to make navy bean soup and Milt Kamen, a comic and a connoisseur if ever I saw one, took one taste and said, "If this is navy bean soup I'll join the army!"

Not all of our guests, for one technical reason or another, get to prepare a recipe on camera. Thank goodness, though, we're still able to learn how they whip together some culinary creation or other because we ask them and they tell us. Result: they provide the show with some unexpected light spots that tickle the funny bones of our viewers although perhaps not their taste buds.

Steve Allen, who is one of the most versatile and talented people I know, everything from author to composer to musician to raconteur, is a good example. I asked Steve for a recipe and this is what he said:

"The only recipe I ever created was one for meatball soup, something I dreamed up several years ago in New York when I discovered nothing much available in the kitchen except a few cans of soup and a pound or two of hamburger.

"You roll the hamburger into small balls which are then fried in a pan.

"As for the soup, mix one can of cream of asparagus with one can of split pea.

"To liven the soup up a bit, add a dash of Worcestershire sauce, then soy sauce.

"Then place several of the fried meatballs in a bowl and pour the soup over them."

It sounded all right but, obviously, I wanted to know how it tastes. To which, Steve delivered this punch line:

"I don't know, because then I go out and eat at the nearest restaurant!"

Well, maybe Steve Allen says he's hesitant about eating his own meatball soup but not us, not us cooking connoisseurs on *The Mike Douglas Show*. Our viewers let us know in letters by the thousands when we have the germ of a good recipe.

So we delivered, verbatim, Steve's rough recipe to the ARA test kitchens, where all the recipes in this book were whipped into working order, because we knew that Carol Walek, the cute little boss lady there, can do wonders with all sorts of oddball ideas. And once again Carol came through. You'll find the recipe on page 45.

Another star who is guaranteed to produce yuks without end, and in the most unexpected places, is Phyllis Diller. She's quite a cook herself, but no one would ever know it from the names she gives to some of her concoctions.

"Will you favor us with a recipe?" I asked her one day.

"Of course," she said.

"Good," I said, "what do you call it?"

"Garbage soup," she said.

"Sounds awful," I said, "for heaven's sake, what do you put into it?"

"Anything at all," she said. "It always has seven cloves of garlic, a large onion, two carrots, two stalks of celery and a bunch of parsley, all of them all chopped up; plus a large can of tomatoes, a can of red kidney beans, salt, pepper and Parmesan cheese. Then I fill a pot half full of water or juices in which vegetables have cooked during the week. I bring it to a boil, add soupbones and any leftover meat that I have lying around and let it boil for an hour and a half. Then I add the chopped vegetables and all of the week's leftovers including spaghetti, sour cream, baked potatoes, you know, Mike, all the things that collect in the icebox and you hate to throw them out. I let the whole mess simmer until tender and then I dare the kids to come and eat."

"Phyllis," I said, "the kids would have to take a dare to eat anything like that. Isn't there anything that you leave out?"

"Of course," she said. "I'd never dream of adding pickles and Jell-O. They'd ruin the taste!"

You won't find the recipe for Phyllis Diller's garbage soup anywhere in this book because Carol Walek spent two days trying and every time she tried she came up with something different.

Finally she threw in the towel ("And I don't mean into the soup," she told me) because, she explained, "There always comes a time when even a test kitchen runs out of leftovers." Which just goes to show that even a home economist-dietitian can be something of a comedienne, too. Carol, by the way, looks more like a Hollywood star than she does a culinary expert but more about her later.

Nor will you find the recipe for Mrs. Mary Haines's cookies in this book, although they did contribute to an extremely heartwarming episode on *The Mike Douglas Show* one week when Trini Lopez was my co-host.

Trini was telling us about his boyhood in Dallas, how he many times was on the verge of dropping out of high school, but how one of his teachers praised his singing voice and told him he could go far if only he would continue his schooling.

"She kept me on the right road," Trini said.

"Do you remember who that teacher was?" I asked.

"How can I ever forget," he said, "her name is Mary Haines."

That was the cue for Mrs. Haines, a lovely gray-haired lady, to walk on and what a surprise reunion it was for Trini, who had had no idea that we were flying her up from Dallas to meet him in Philadelphia.

They talked about those days at the N. R. Crozier Technical High School, there were some tears, and then Mrs. Haines surprised Trini a second time by handing him a box of her homemade cookies, the same cookies she often had made for him while keeping him from becoming a high school dropout.

Then Mrs. Haines went off and we went on with the show and soon it was time for Adela Rogers St. John, one of my favorite authors and another fine lady, to come on.

We greeted each other and then Adela said:

"Mike, before we say another word, I must tell you that Mrs. Haines promised me a cookie if I do one thing . . ."

"What is that?" I asked.

"I must tell your listeners that Mrs. Haines does not teach in Crozier High anymore. She now teaches in North Dallas High School. Now, I've said it. Now I've earned my cookie."

As I said, it was an extremely heartwarming episode. But it did not end there. We were deluged with requests for Mrs. Haines's cookie recipe in the mails that followed. So we got in touch with her in Dallas and asked for the recipe. But we never did receive it and therefore we cannot include it in this book.

Sorry.

Guests on our show don't have to be a Mary Haines to provide a tear, or a Phyllis Diller to provide a laugh.

Take Maureen Stapleton and E. G. Marshall. Their fame comes far more from straight acting than from comedy. Still, they know the value of a yuk ending on a show like mine.

They were co-starring in the Broadway hit *Plaza Suite*, but took time out from a rugged schedule to hop down to Philadelphia. We went through the usual conversational bits, then I asked E. G. Marshall what the initials stood for and he wouldn't tell, not even when the studio audience tried to guess.

So then, knowing he is a health food nut, I asked him to favor us with a recipe.

"I came prepared," he said, "to demonstrate one that's guaranteed to make a man of you."

We moved over to the roll-around counter that passes for a kitchen on *The Mike Douglas Show* and E. G. Marshall demonstrated with Maureen Stapleton and me as interested onlookers.

"First," he said, "you take a container of plain yogurt, then you add to it a tablespoon of wheat germ, a tablespoon of brewer's yeast and two tablespoons of chopped lettuce. Then you mix it together well and eat. Like this."

He took a taste, smacked his lips, hefted back his shoulders like he'd just grown ten feet tall, and said, "Umm, that's good. Here, Maureen, you try it."

Miss Stapleton, the fine Broadway actress, very delicate and every inch a lady, took a taste. Very delicate, very feminine. She swallowed and just as she did, somewhere offstage, someone let out with a fierce Tarzan yell, put up to it by Mr. E. G. Marshall, the supposedly straight actor!

Our show's kitchen capers, as you can see, have unexpected ingredients popping up all over. Not only are there unlisted additions sounding off backstage, but we even have them popping up in the finished recipe.

One such event occurred when Barbara Rush showed us how she prepares Rock Cornish hen baked in a hard shell of salt.

We don't have the time, as everyone knows, to start from scratch and do the whole recipe on the air. So the actual baking was done long before showtime. Barbara demonstrated only how to prepare the recipe, then reached under the counter and brought out the finished product.

I handed her a hammer to crack the shell so we all could see what the baked bird looked like. She gave it a whack, the shell broke apart and out flew a live dove! The recipe is on page 122, but without the shell; one live dove is enough.

A somewhat similar finale came the time Bobbie Gentry, the fine gal singer from down South, showed us how her grandma bakes corn bread. She took us through the recipe, step by step, then produced an already-baked loaf, cut into it and ran into a whole ear of corn, put there by Grady Nutt, who is just as much a Southerner as she is but much more of a kibitzer.

We've had a great many Southerners on *The Mike Douglas Show* and it's amazing how many of them will favor our viewers with their recipes for corn bread. Bobbie Gentry is one of them and Grandpa Jones and Minnie Pearl, both great Country and Western entertainers, are two more. You'll find their recipes in the Bread Section. Compare them, note the differences between them and see if you don't agree that they are all good.

Recipes for Caesar salad also come regularly from our guests. Not only will you find my recipe in the salad section . . . thanks to my wife, Genevieve, who carefully recorded the amounts of everything that I put into it the last time I made it . . . but you'll also find versions from Shelley Winters, Michael O'Shea and maybe one or two others, too. And all of them different, especially Shelley's.

Hers, you might say, not only is different, it's unique. Really unique. Not because three heads of lettuce go into her Caesar salad— romaine, iceberg and Boston—not because she washes them, breaks them up, shakes them dry and then stores them in the refrigerator.

But because she does all this inside a pillowcase! (A clean one, of course!)

I'll say this for Shelley's methods, her lettuce ends up nice and crisp, which is a claim that I cannot make for Pat O'Brien's lettuce, mainly because his recipe is for a wilted lettuce salad!

But enough of all that chatter about the quips, the quirks, the tricks, that our viewers saw, heard, learned from or laughed at during cooking sessions on *The Mike Douglas Show*. Except that I must caution users of this book to check the number of portions they'll end up with when they prepare one of its recipes. I say that because the variation is great, anywhere from one to twenty.

Twenty! That's how many servings Betty Hughes can get out of her recipe for Irish Beef Stew Pie that you'll find on page 89. But then she has to cook in big quantities because she has ten kids running around her State House.

I'm awfully proud to have had the wife of New Jersey's Governor Richard J. Hughes as our guest quite often, and what a delight she is. And that goes too for the wives of so many other men in high office, Muriel Humphrey, Lady Bird Johnson and Patricia Nixon, to name just three. You'll find recipes from all of them in this book and I want to thank them from the bottom of my heart for being so kind to Mother Dowd's boy, Michael.

I want to thank Connie Francis, too, for bringing her mother along to show us how to make Eggplant Parmesan. A fine lady she was.

Thanks, Mom.

II

And Now for the Recipes

Thank You, Carol Walek

We come now to the meat and potato portion of *The Mike Douglas Cookbook*. The one hundred and fifty or so recipes that follow are what this book is all about.

Here's where Carol Walek, the young lady I made mention of a few pages back, took charge, treating each recipe just as she treats every recipe with which the company for whom she works feeds something like five million people a day.

Carol is Director of Standards for ARA Services, a gigantic food complex of which it's a good bet you've never heard. It's also a good bet that at some time or other you've eaten their food because, besides feeding those five million hungry Americans every day, ARA also provides coffee-break snacks and food-vending machine provender for I don't know how many more millions every day.

But none of them eats a thing that hasn't first been tested to perfection by Carol and her test-kitchen crew. ARA employs more than three hundred dietitians in various locations around the United States and Canada, some in hospitals, some in colleges, some in company kitchens, some in public restaurants. They're given pretty much free rein as to what to serve and when to serve it, but with one important proviso: that they confine their daily choices to the fifteen hundred basic recipes that originated in those test kitchens and that Carol and her staff seek constantly to improve.

It was this background, this know-how, that Carol brought to the recipes in this book. We knew that every recipe would have to be carefully tested when we decided there should be such a book; we knew that most of them would have to be whipped into working order because, let's face it, guests on *The Mike Douglas Show* are far from specific when they tell how much of this or that ingredient should go into a recipe, or when it should go in, or how it should go in.

So, then, the next question: Who should do the testing? Who should turn a culinary idea into a full-fledged working recipe that any housewife could with confidence add to her kitchen repertoire? It would have to be someone professional, someone unimpeachable, someone whose accreditation would speak for itself.

The word went out. We searched the country high and low. And, lo, we found what we were looking for right here in Philadelphia, just a mile or so from Westinghouse's KYW studios that are the home of *The Mike Douglas Show*.

Philadelphia, as it turned out, is also the home of ARA Services, a corporate giant which, through all of its many subsidiary affiliates, takes in somewhat more than $475,000,000 a year just by serving food to hungry Americans.

We learned that ARA operates everything from employee cafeterias to executive dining rooms for about five hundred industrial giants such as General Motors, U.S. Steel and IBM. We learned that ARA feeds our space scientists at Cape Kennedy. We learned that ARA owns and operates such restaurants as the Promenade Cafe at New York's Lincoln Center. We learned that ARA was in Mexico to feed ten thousand athletes from all over the world three energy-building meals a day at the 1968 Olympic Games. We learned that ARA has had several command performances at the White House. We learned that ARA operates the food service in thousands of hospitals, secondary schools and colleges.

We learned that ARA even owns the food-vending machines just outside my office door!

So we caught a cab and went down to ARA's kitchens and there we met Carol Walek, a blonde bundle of charm who looks like anything but a Director of Standards for such a complex. Carol was graduated with honors in 1958 from the University of Connecticut with a B.S. degree in foods and nutrition.

She is a member of the American Dietetic Association and of the American Home Economics Association. She was, a year or so ago, chairman of the Philadelphia Chapter of Home Economists in Business.

We learned that ARA and Carol were what we'd searched the country for. And here they both were volunteering to baby every recipe in this book into a delectable dish that meets all of their professional standards. What's more, Carol volunteered to test every one of them personally and she did, even adding five or six of her own because she felt that *The Mike Douglas Cookbook* could use them.

Carol Walek, we thank you!

(And we thank too your secretary, Helen Master, for keeping the recipes rolling to us.)

*

Appetizers
and
Beverages

---

*

SEBASTIAN CABOT'S
Avocado Surprise Yvonne

CRÊPES:

⅔ cup flour
1 Tb. sugar
Pinch salt
2 eggs

2 egg yolks
1¾ cups milk
2 Tbs. melted butter

Sift dry ingredients together. Beat whole eggs and yolks until frothy. Add eggs and milk to dry ingredients. Stir until smooth. Add butter. Stir until well combined. Set aside for 2 hours.

In a 5- or 6-inch frying pan, heat 1 tsp. of sweet butter over moderate heat until butter foams. Pour 1½ Tbs. batter into pan. Rotate pan quickly to spread batter as thinly and evenly as possible. Cook crêpe 1 minute on each side. Stack crêpes on top of each other until all are done.

GUACAMOLE SALAD:

2 large very ripe avo-
    cados
¼ cup grated onion

1 Tb. fresh lemon juice
1 tsp. salt
4 to 6 drops Tabasco

Cut avocado in half. Remove pit. Spoon out pulp and mash. Add remaining ingredients. Whip into fine paste. Cover and refrigerate until needed.

CHEESE SAUCE:

3 cups half & half
1 cup (4 oz.) finely
    shredded Cheddar
    cheese

3 egg yolks, beaten
¾ tsp. salt
⅛ tsp. white pepper

Place cream over hot water in double boiler. When hot, gradually add cheese, stirring constantly. When completely melted add equal amount of hot mixture to eggs and mix well. Add egg mixture to cheese mixture. Add salt and pepper and blend well. Cook until thickened, approximately 5 minutes, stirring constantly. Remove immediately from heat.

TO ASSEMBLE:

16 crêpes	2 cups Guacamole salad
½ lb. thinly sliced Nova Scotia lox	3 cups cheese sauce

Preheat broiler.

On each crêpe place 1 slice lox and 1 tablespoon Guacamole. Roll each crêpe, tucking in ends. Arrange 1 layer deep in a 9-inch square greased glass casserole. Pour cream sauce over crêpes. Broil 4 inches from heat 4 to 5 minutes or until bubbly and golden brown.

Place 2 crêpes on each plate with sauce. Decorate with left-over guacamole salad that has been forced through a pastry tube.
Serves 8.

GENEVIEVE'S

Broiled Grapefruit

2 grapefruit (room temperature)	3 Tbs. sugar
4 tsps. butter	1 tsp. cinnamon

Preheat broiler.

Cut grapefruit in half crosswise. Cut sections to loosen; remove center. Fill each center with 1 tsp. butter. Combine sugar and cinnamon. Sprinkle 2½ tsps. of cinnamon mixture over each grapefruit half.

Broil 4 inches from flame 8 to 10 minutes or until grapefruit top is browned and grapefruit is bubbly.
Serves 4.

PEGGY KING'S
Guacamole Holiday Dip

2 large very ripe avo-
  cados
3 Tbs. minced Bermuda
  onion
2 Tbs. mayonnaise

2 Tbs. lemon juice
1 tsp. paprika
1 tsp. seasoned salt
3 to 4 drops Tabasco
¼ tsp. Worcestershire sauce

Cut avocados in half. Remove pits. Spoon out pulp and mash. Add remaining ingredients and whip into fine paste. Dip discolors when held. If to be stored, place pit in center and cover tightly with plastic wrap.

Serve with corn chips.

Makes 2 cups.

GENEVIÈVE'S
Snails

¼ cup melted butter
½ clove garlic, minced
1 fresh shallot, chopped
  very fine

¼ cup pernod or white
  wine
2 dozen snails and shells

Preheat oven to 425° F.

Combine butter, garlic, shallot and pernod or wine. Remove snails from shells. Place 1 tsp. of the mixture in each snail shell. Replace snails in shell. Bake 10 to 15 minutes or until hot and bubbly. Serve immediately.

Serves 4.

NOTE: The Geneviève to whom we are indebted for this recipe is the French personality and not my wife Genevieve. Their names are spelled the same but pronounced differently.

LOUIS NYE'S

Steak Tar Tare

1½ lbs. freshly ground
  lean beef
1 Tb. hot prepared
  mustard
1 tsp. salt
½ tsp. Worcestershire
  sauce

1½ cups finely chopped
  Bermuda or Spanish
  onion
3 egg yolks
2 hard-cooked eggs,
  chopped
1 Tb. chopped onion

Combine meat, mustard, salt, Worcestershire, onion and egg yolks. Mix well. Shape into loaf. Place on serving platter. Garnish with chopped eggs and onion.

Serve with rye bread.

Serves 8 to 12.

NOTE: Louis, as you know, is a very funny fellow. But what you don't know is that he's also a stickler (1) about how Tar Tare is spelled; (2) that the rye bread be sliced thin, and (3) if you don't like rye, use pumpernickel, which he spells pumpernickle. Who knows, maybe he's right!

GENEVIEVE'S

Holiday Eggnog

12 eggs, separated
2 cups sugar
Fifth of favorite whiskey
  or rum
Few dashes bitters
  (optional)

1 pt. whipping cream,
  whipped
1 pt. milk
Nutmeg to garnish

In 4-quart mixing bowl, beat yolks until light and fluffy. Add sugar and beat until lemon colored. Add liquor, bitters, whipped cream and milk. Mix until smooth. Cover and refrigerate until serving time. (Do not hold more than 12 hours.) Beat whites until stiff but not dry. In punch bowl fold yolk mixture into whites. Sprinkle with nutmeg to garnish.

Makes 6 quarts.

SMILIN' JACK SMITH'S

Four O'Clock Pickup Drink *

8 oz. fresh orange juice	1 Tb. honey
1 egg yolk	1 Tb. plain gelatin
1 Tb. wheat germ	(1 packet)

Combine all ingredients in blender. Add ice if desired. Blend on high speed 1 minute.

Serves 1.

CAROL WALEK'S

Crab Meat Puffs

8 slices thinly sliced bread	1 cup flaked crab meat
4 tsps. butter	1 cup mayonnaise
	2 egg whites, stiffly beaten

Preheat broiler.

Cut bread into ¾-inch rounds. Sauté in butter in skillet. Place in refrigerator until chilled. Combine crab meat and mayonnaise. Fold into stiffly beaten egg whites. Put 1 tsp. of the mixture on each toast round. Broil immediately until lightly browned or freeze immediately, before egg white collapses.

Makes about 60.

To freeze, place on cookie sheet and freeze. When frozen, place in plastic bag; seal and store in freezer.

* It's a great breakfast drink, too, no matter what time you eat breakfast.

To broil, place on cookie sheet and broil 4 inches from heat 5 to 7 minutes or until lightly browned.

CAROL WALEK'S

Champagne Punch

1 qt. fresh strawberries	2 bottles Rhine wine
¼ cup sugar	2 bottles champagne
Juice of 1 lemon	

Hull and wash strawberries. Place in punch bowl or other glass container that will hold at least 4 quarts. Sprinkle strawberries with sugar and lemon juice. Add Rhine wine. Chill 3 to 4 hours or overnight. Just before serving add champagne.

To add a festive and decorative touch, make an ice mold with strawberries frozen into it.

Makes 4 quarts or 32 servings, 4 oz. each.

*

Soups

---

*

MURIEL HUMPHREY'S
Beef Soup

1½ lbs. beef shanks	1 cup finely chopped celery
2 tsps. salt	1 cup finely chopped
½ tsp. pepper	cabbage
2 bay leaves	½ Tb. Worcestershire sauce
3 qts. hot water	2½ cups Italian style to-
1½ cups sliced carrots,	matoes, crushed; or
¼-inch thick	20-oz. can
½ cup finely chopped	
onion	

Place meat and seasonings in 4-quart pot. Add water. Bring to a boil. Add remaining ingredients. Cover and simmer 2½ to 3 hours or until meat separates from bone. Remove bone and bay leaves. Cut meat into bite-sized pieces. Add meat.
Serves 4 to 6.

MARIE McDONALD'S
Corn Soup

4 cups diced potatoes,	2 cups cream style corn, or
½-inch cubes	1-lb. can
2 cups diced onions,	¼ cup butter
½-inch pieces	¼ tsp. white pepper
2 cups water	1 qt. milk
1 Tb. salt	¼ cup chopped parsley

Cook potatoes and onions in boiling salted water in 4-quart saucepan 15 to 20 minutes or until done. Add remaining ingredients. Simmer gently 5 minutes.
Makes 6 bowls of soup.

NOTE: Marie McDonald is gone now and I'd like to tell you about a side of her that was never made known to the public.

Far from being the somewhat dumb blonde type, I found her to be extremely warm, kind and compassionate during the week that she was my co-host on *The Mike Douglas Show*. Much, I must admit, to my surprise, because until then all I knew about her was what I saw on the screen or read in the newspapers and magazines.

There was a blind woman, a mother of four, not a woman of means, on the show one day that week and that specifically is when it was brought home to me just how kindhearted a lady Marie McDonald was. Although she could not see, our guest was a marvelous seamstress, making just about everything imaginable for her home. Curtains, pillow slips, tablecloths, everything . . . including all of her children's clothes!

That's why she was there: to show how she does it. My staff had borrowed a sewing machine (to me it looked like a Cadillac) on which she could demonstrate her skills. Marie introduced her, she sat down at the machine, looked it over carefully with her fingers, tried it, got to know it, then exclaimed: "Oh, this is the most marvelous sewing machine I've ever seen!"

Tears filled Marie's eyes and they remained there all the while the blind lady sat at that machine showing all of us, the sighted, how seemingly easy it is to sew or, the deeper message, how to do anything that we set our minds to do if only we will use the skills that God gave us and not allow ourselves to drown in self-pity.

Then we were off the air and Marie turned to me and said: "Oh, Mike, I must give that wonderful lady that sewing machine. Please help me buy it for her."

So someone on my staff checked with the store from which it came and was told it would cost $375. I was shocked.

"Marie," I said, "You can't spend all that money. You're only getting one thousand dollars for the whole week and at that rate you'll go home broke."

"I don't care, Mike," she replied. "That lady must have that sewing machine and I am going to get it for her."

And she did.

STEVE ALLEN'S

Meatball Soup

½ lb. ground beef
½ tsp. salt
⅛ tsp. pepper
1 can cream of aspara-
    gus soup, 10¼ ozs.

1 can split pea soup,
    10¼ ozs.
¼ tsp. Worcestershire
    sauce
Soy sauce as needed

Combine ground beef, salt and pepper. Shape into ½-inch meatballs. Sauté over moderate heat, turning as necessary, until well browned.

Make soups as directed on can, using water to reconstitute. Combine meatballs and soup. Add a dash of Worcestershire. Serve soy sauce as an accompaniment.

Serves 6.

GENEVIEVE'S

Onion Soup

5 cups yellow onion
    slices, ⅛-inch thick
    (1½ lbs. as pur-
    chased)
3 Tbs. butter
1 Tb. oil
1 tsp. salt
¼ tsp. sugar

3 Tbs. flour
2 qts. beef broth
8 buttered toast rounds or
    buttered toasted French
    bread slices
¾ cup grated Parmesan
    cheese

Separate onions into rings. Cook in butter and oil *slowly* in covered 3-quart saucepan for 15 minutes or until transparent. Remove lid. Add salt and sugar. Cook over moderate heat stirring constantly until onions are a deep golden brown, approximately 35 minutes. Add flour gradually, stirring constantly. Cook 10 minutes longer. Add broth. Bring to a boil.

Place a toast round in each bowl. Pour soup over toast. Pass cheese in bowl.

Serves 8.

PAT SUZUKI'S

Su-Zoup-Ki

You'll need individual ramekins or ovenproof bowls for this delightful and interesting soup.

4 eggs
1⅔ cups chicken broth
¼ lb. ground beef
½ tsp. salt
⅛ tsp. pepper
⅛ tsp. oregano

6 scallions cut into ¼-inch rings
½ cup thawed frozen chopped spinach
½ cup thawed frozen peas

Preheat oven to 400° F.

In mixing bowl, beat eggs until foamy. Add broth; mix well. Set aside. Combine ground beef and seasonings. Shape into ½-inch meatballs.

Divide meatballs among 4 ramekins. Top with rounded tablespoon each of scallions, spinach and peas. Pour ⅔ cup egg mixture over this. Cover ramekins.

Bake in pan with ½-inch boiling water in it for 10 to 12 minutes or until egg mixture has a golden custardlike consistency.

Serves 4.

NOTE: Mixture continues to cook after removing from oven so if soup is to stand after cooking, shorten cooking time.

*

Try This
in Your
Funk & Wagnalls

*

BENNETT CERF'S

Random Recipe

If this recipe doesn't look like, or read like, any other recipe in *The Mike Douglas Cookbook* you'll soon know why. It came our way the week that Bennett Cerf (publisher, pundit, television personality and definitely *not* a cook) was my co-host. As it does to all other co-hosts, there came the time when Bennett was asked to prepare a recipe before the cameras so that all America could see and hear and learn.

That's when *I* learned.

Bennett donned apron and chef's hat, stepped manfully up to the worktable that serves as our kitchen and said:

"Here now is my recipe for making Corn Flakes with Cream:

"Open one package of Corn Flakes along the dotted line and pour the contents into a large bowl. Add cream and serve."

I was shocked.

"Is that all?" I exclaimed. "Is that all you're going to make?"

"That is all," he replied. "This is my entire cooking repertoire at the moment, but I hope to enlarge same as soon as I learn how to open an egg!"

That, of course, is something to look forward to and I promise to keep you informed. Meantime, though, the Random House proprietor's recipe for Corn Flakes with Cream posed a problem. How to categorize it? Certainly not under meats, or poultry or appetizers or salads or some other such prosaic classification.

So, making use of words immortalized by Rowan and Martin, we devised a classification never before used in *any* cookbook: Try This in Your Funk & Wagnalls.

We did in my house and do you know what?

It tasted just like the Corn Flakes and Cream that Mother used to make!

Salads

CAROL WALEK'S

Coddled Eggs

This recipe may seem out of place in this, the salad section. But, since the first few recipes are for Caesar salad and since all of them call for coddled eggs, we think it's highly appropriate here. That's because if you ask any three people how they coddle an egg, chances are you'll get either three different versions or else at least one of the three will ask, "What *is* a coddled egg?"

It's important, therefore, to know exactly how Carol Walek, the gal who tested all of these recipes, coddles an egg. So here's how:

Remove one large egg from refrigerator and allow to stand until at room temperature, about ½ hour. Meantime bring enough water to cover to a rapid boil. Lower room-temperature egg into water, making certain it's covered with water, reduce heat to just under the boiling point and cook for one minute. Then remove from water and set aside until needed. The egg is not "set"— yolks are runny and the whites are creamy.

CAESAR DOUGLAS

Salad

1 clove garlic, cut in
    quarters
1 tsp. salt
½ tsp. fresh ground
    pepper
⅔ cup olive oil
2 eggs, coddled
    (p. 53)
2 heads romaine lettuce
    (approximately 1 lb.
    as purchased)

1 head iceberg lettuce
1 large ripe avocado
2 Tbs. anchovy paste
2 lemons, juiced
2 Tbs. red wine vinegar
⅔ cup croutons
½ cup freshly grated Par-
    mesan cheese

Marinate garlic with salt and pepper in olive oil several hours or overnight. Remove garlic. Coddle eggs for 1 minute. Set aside until needed.

Wash and dry lettuce. Break into bite-sized pieces. Refrigerate in plastic bag until needed. Cut avocado in half. Remove pit. Spoon out pulp. Mash in large wooden salad bowl. Add anchovy, lemon juice, vinegar and oil mixture. Mix well. Add greens. Toss lightly. Add croutons, cheese and coddled eggs. Toss lightly again.

Serves 12.

MICHAEL O'SHEA'S

Caesar Salad

1 clove garlic, sliced
   lengthwise in
   quarters
⅓ cup olive oil
1 egg, coddled (p. 53)
1 head romaine lettuce
   (approximately 1 lb.
   as purchased)
2 Tbs. vinegar

1 lemon, juiced
Salt and freshly ground
   pepper to taste
¼ cup Parmesan cheese
Dash Worcestershire sauce
⅓ cup croutons
1 can rolled anchovies,
   2 ozs.

Marinate garlic in oil overnight.

Coddle egg for 1 minute. Set aside until needed. Wash and dry lettuce. Refrigerate in plastic bag until needed.

Break lettuce into salad bowl. Drizzle garlic oil, vinegar and lemon juice over lettuce. Add coddled egg. Sprinkle with salt and freshly ground pepper to taste, Parmesan cheese and dash of Worcestershire. Roll-toss six times. Add croutons and toss once. Serve on chilled plates. Garnish with anchovies.

Serves 6.

SHELLEY WINTERS'

Caesar Salad

1 head romaine lettuce
1 head iceberg lettuce
1 head Boston lettuce
2 eggs, coddled
(p. 53)
½ cup red wine vinegar
½ cup olive oil
1 can anchovies
(include oil), 2 ozs.
1 Tb. dry mustard

1½ tsps. Worcestershire
sauce
2 lemons, juiced
1 clove garlic, crushed
1 tsp. freshly ground
pepper
1 cup croutons
½ cup freshly ground
Parmesan cheese

Wash romaine, iceberg and Boston lettuce. Break up and place in a pillowcase and shake dry. Store in refrigerator until needed.

Coddle eggs for 1 minute. Combine eggs, vinegar, oil, anchovies, mustard, Worcestershire, lemon juice, garlic and pepper. Beat well.

Place lettuce in large wooden bowl. Sprinkle with croutons and cheese. Pour dressing over it. Toss gently with one hand.

Serves 12.

AL MARTINO'S

Hearts of Romaine with Anchovy Dressing

8 to 10 hearts of
romaine lettuce
(yellow part only)
8 anchovy fillets
(include packing
liquor)

¼ cup red wine vinegar
2 Tbs. herb-flavored bread
crumbs

Wash lettuce; drain and chill.

Mash anchovy fillets. Add oil, vinegar and crumbs. Mix until smooth.

Place lettuce in large salad bowl. Pour dressing over greens. Toss lightly.

Serves 4.

Carol, our food expert, says, "People should eat more raw vegetables and here's a recipe on which they can begin to acquire a taste."

CAROL WALEK'S

Spinach Salad

1 clove garlic, sliced lengthwise in quarters	2 hard-cooked eggs, chopped
¾ cup olive oil	¼ cup sweet Bermuda onion rings, ⅛ inch thick
¼ cup vinegar	
1 lb. spinach	6 slices bacon, cooked, crumbled
Salt and pepper to taste	

Marinate garlic in oil and vinegar overnight. Remove and discard garlic. Wash spinach. Remove stems and discolored parts. Drain. Break into 2-inch pieces in salad bowl. Sprinkle with salt and pepper to taste, eggs, onion and bacon. Pour garlic oil over mixture. Toss lightly. Serve on chilled plates.

Serves 4.

PAT O'BRIEN'S

Wilted Lettuce Salad

1 head romaine lettuce	¼ cup red wine vinegar
6 slices bacon	½ tsp. salt
4 scallions,	¼ tsp. black pepper
finely chopped	2 hard-cooked eggs, sliced
1 tsp. sugar	

Wash lettuce, drain, chill. Break into salad bowl.

Fry bacon until crisp. Remove from pan and drain on absorbent paper. Add scallions, sugar, vinegar, salt and pepper to bacon fat. Bring to a boil.

Pour dressing over lettuce. Cover for 30 seconds. Toss lightly or until lettuce is wilted. Crumble bacon and sprinkle over salad. Garnish with egg slices. Serve immediately.

Serves 4.

NOTE: If lettuce does not wilt, drain dressing from bowl into pan, reheat, pour, and toss again.

GENEVIEVE'S

Honey Dressing

½ cup honey	1 tsp. lemon juice
½ cup salad dressing	½ tsp. paprika
1 tsp. celery seed	

Combine all ingredients. Refrigerate until needed. Serve with fresh fruit salad.

Makes 1 cup.

GENEVIEVE'S

Fruit Salad with Cheese Icing

1 Tb. unflavored gela-
    tin (1 envelope)
¼ cup cold water
1 cup milk
1 Tb. butter
6 ozs. soft cream cheese

1 can pineapple chunks,
    30 ozs.
1 can pears, 30 ozs.
2 pkgs. (3 oz.) lemon-
    flavored gelatin dessert
2 cups boiling water

Soften gelatin in cold water. Set aside. Combine milk, butter and cream cheese in saucepan. Bring to a boil stirring constantly. Add softened gelatin; stir until dissolved. Pour into 10-inch angel cake pan or ring mold. Chill until set.

Drain fruit and cut pears into ¾-inch chunks. Save juices. Dissolve flavored gelatin in boiling water. Add enough cold water to juices to make 2 cups. Add this to gelatin mixture. Chill until partially set. Fold in fruit. Pour on top of cheese mixture. Chill until set.

Unmold on bed of lettuce. To serve, cut as you would cake. Serves 8.

SAMMY DAVIS, JR.'S

Salad

1 clove garlic	6 ripe olives, pitted and
1 head Romaine lettuce	shredded
2 tomatoes, quartered	2 green peppers, cut across
3 to 4 Tbs. wheat germ	in rings

Rub the inside of a wooden salad bowl with the garlic clove; discard garlic.

Wash the lettuce; dry thoroughly with a lint-free cloth. Tear into medium-sized pieces, and put into the bowl. Add quartered tomatoes, wheat germ, and dressing (below); toss well. Decorate top with green pepper rings.

Serves 4.

DRESSING:

¼ cup salad oil	½ tsp. lemon juice
¼ cup red wine vinegar	½ tsp. salt
½ tsp. Worcestershire	⅛ tsp. black pepper,
sauce	freshly ground

Combine all ingredients in a jar. Cover and shake well. Makes ½ cup.

Omelets, Fondues, Blintzes, and Such

GENEVIEVE'S
Eggs Basted Easily

2 Tbs. butter   2 Tbs. hot water
4 eggs

Melt butter over low heat in frying pan. Break eggs into pan. When white begins to cook, add water. Cover and cook 1 to 2 minutes or until doneness desired.
Serves 2.

JIMMY NELSON'S
California Breakfast

4 sausage links   4 to 5 drops Maggi
1 Tb. minced onion   seasoning
Cold water to cover   ¾ tsp. salt
8 eggs   ½ tsp. sugar
½ cup milk   2 Tbs. butter
2 drops Tabasco

Preheat oven to 350° F.

Bake sausage in shallow pan until well browned (about 45 minutes). Remove from fat. Drain on absorbent paper. Cut into ¼-inch slices.

Soak onion in water 5 minutes. Drain. Whip eggs with fork. Add milk, seasonings, sugar, drained onions and sausage slices.

Melt butter in skillet.

Pour egg mixture into skillet and cook over low heat, stirring occasionally, until thickened but still moist. 5 to 8 minutes.
Serves 8.

NOTE: Ventriloquist Jimmy Nelson created this recipe one time upon returning to his Florida home from a California engagement (accompanied of course by his inseparable companion, Farfel) and discovering that his three older sons had not been eating their breakfast eggs. Now they eat their eggs, and so do Son Number Four and their two sisters.

PAT MORRISSEY'S
Cheese Blintzes

6 ozs. cream cheese,
  softened
¼ tsp. salt
Dash white pepper
6 slices fresh thinly
  sliced white bread

1 egg, beaten
2 Tbs. butter
½ cup sour cream

Whip cheese, salt and pepper together.

Remove crust from bread. Roll each piece of bread with rolling pin until flat. Place 2 Tbs. cheese along center third of bread. Fold in thirds envelope style. Pinch ends together. Coat bread with beaten egg. Fry over moderate heat in butter in skillet until golden brown. Serve with sour cream and jelly.

Serves 2.

SKITCH HENDERSON'S
Eggs Orange

4 eggs
3 Tbs. butter
1 Tb. frozen orange
  juice concentrate

¼ tsp. seasoned salt
½ tsp. parsley
2 English muffins, split and
  toasted

Fry eggs gently in 2 Tbs. butter in skillet. Remove eggs and keep hot. Add remaining butter and brown. Add orange juice, slowly so it does not spatter, seasoned salt, and parsley. Heat. Put eggs on English muffin. Pour 1 tablespoon sauce over each egg.

Serves 2.

DOROTHY DANDRIDGE'S
Emotional Omelet

OMELET:

Make omelet twice. Use 6 eggs each time and a 10-inch omelet pan.

6 eggs
2 Tbs. cold water
¾ tsp. onion salt

Pinch of pepper
1½ Tbs. butter

Combine eggs, water, onion salt and pepper in bowl. Beat with fork until slightly frothy on top. Melt butter in hot pan. As soon as butter foams, add eggs. Move pan back and forth and at same time stir eggs in circle 8 to 10 times around.

Smooth top of omelet with fork. When edges are done but center still creamy, fold omelet in thirds and turn out onto platter. Serve with sauce. Or spread half of sauce over half of egg in pan and fold over. Garnish with parsley. Serve with a baked tomato.

Serves 6.

SAUCE:

4 slices bacon
½ cup finely chopped
   onion
½ cup finely chopped
   green pepper
½ cup finely chopped
   celery
2 cloves garlic, minced

1½ Tbs. tomato paste
1 lb. ground round
¼ lb. bulk pork sausage
1 tsp. seasoned salt
½ tsp. garlic powder
1 tsp. chili powder
2 Tbs. dry sherry

Sauté bacon until crisp. Remove and drain on absorbent paper. Discard half the bacon drippings. Add vegetables and tomato paste to the rest. Cover and cook over low heat 15 minutes or until vegetables are tender, stirring occasionally. Add remaining ingredients except wine. Cook, stirring constantly, until meat is well browned. Skim off excess fat. Add wine, crumble bacon into mixture, and stir. Set aside.

NOTE: Sauce may be prepared ahead. It should, however, be hot at serving time.

GYPSY ROSE LEE'S

Linger Longer Omelet

¼ lb. Italian link sausage sliced ¼ inch thick

¼ green pepper cut into ¼-inch strips

1 Tb. olive oil

½ cup sliced onion, ⅛ inch thick

1 small potato, peeled, sliced ¼ inch thick

½ tsp. salt

1 slice prosciutto cut into ½-inch strips

1 tomato, peeled and sliced ¼ inch thick

2 Tbs. chopped pimiento

6 eggs

1 Tb. chopped parsley

1 Tb. olive oil

Garlic

Sauté sausage and pepper in 1 Tb. oil over low heat 4 to 5 minutes or until sausage begins to brown. Add onion, potato and salt. Cover and continue to cook, stirring gently occasionally, 5 to 10 minutes or until onions are transparent. Add ham, tomato and pimiento. Cook until tender. Drain excess fat.

Break eggs into mixing bowl. Add parsley. Beat with fork until frothy. Add sausage mixture.

In 10-inch omelet pan, heat remaining Tb. olive oil. Sauté garlic until it browns. Discard. Add egg mixture.

Move pan back and forth and at same time stir eggs in circle 6 to 8 times. Smooth top of omelet with fork. When edges are done but center still creamy, fold omelet in thirds.

Serves 2 to 3.

PRUDENCE PENNY'S

Omelet with Bel Paese Cheese & Red Caviar

¼ cup finely chopped
    onion
1 Tb. butter
6 eggs
2 Tbs. cold water
1½ Tbs. butter

¼ lb. Bel Paese cheese,
    cut into ¼-inch cubes
Celery or pepper flakes
2-oz. jar red salmon caviar
    —cold

Sauté onion in 1 Tb. butter until transparent. Set aside.

Combine eggs and water in bowl. Beat with fork until frothy on top.

Melt 1½ Tbs. butter in hot 10-inch omelet pan. As soon as butter foams, add eggs. Move pan back and forth and at same time stir eggs in circle 8 to 10 times around. Add sautéed onions. Smooth top of omelet. Top with cheese. When edges are done and cheese has melted sprinkle with celery or pepper flakes. Drop dollops of caviar on omelet.

Fold omelet in thirds and serve immediately.

The icy cold caviar contrasts with the hot omelet. Accompany omelet with pepper mill for guests to season to taste.

Serves 2 to 3.

JOANIE SOMMERS'

Pierogi

4 cups sifted flour	1 tsp. salt
1 tsp. salt	Water to cover
4 eggs, slightly beaten	½ cup milk
¾ cup lukewarm water	1½ tsps. salt
8 medium-sized pota-	2½ cups grated Cheddar
toes, peeled and	cheese
quartered	Butter

Sift flour and salt together into mixing bowl. Add eggs and stir with fork until well mixed. Gradually add water and stir until mixture forms a smooth ball (dough should clean the bowl but not be sticky). Turn out dough on very lightly floured board and knead for a few minutes until smooth and elastic. Set aside in floured covered bowl for 30 minutes.

Meanwhile, cook potatoes in salted water to cover 20 to 25 minutes or until tender; drain. Mash. Add milk, salt and cheese and whip until fluffy.

Roll out ¼ the dough to a 16 x 16-inch square. Cut into circles with 2-inch cutter. Fill with 1 tsp. of potato mixture. Moisten edges with water. Fold in half and seal edges. Repeat with remaining dough. Set aside and dry 2 hours on floured pan. Drop pierogi into boiling salted water. Reduce heat and simmer 10 to 15 minutes or until tender. Remove from cooking liquid with slotted spoon.

Melt butter in large frying pan. Over moderate heat, saute pierogi until slightly browned. Serve with sour cream.

Serves 8.

CAROL LAWRENCE'S

Precious Flower Egg

¼ cup dried Chinese
mushrooms
2 Tbs. oil
½ tsp. salt
½ cup bamboo shoots,
⅛-inch slices
¼ cup snow peas,
⅛-inch slices

½ cup onion, ⅛-inch slices
¼ lb. thinly sliced barbe-
cued pork or ham cut
into ½-inch strips
6 eggs, well beaten
¼ tsp. monosodium
glutamate

Soak mushrooms in cold water to cover 10 minutes or until tender. Drain. Slice thin. Heat oil and salt in skillet over high heat. Add mushrooms and remaining ingredients except eggs and monosodium glutamate. Cook quickly, tossing lightly, 5 minutes or until vegetables are almost done. Reduce heat. Add eggs and scramble gently until doneness desired.

Serves 4.

ANN MILLER'S

Cheese Soufflé

¼ cup butter
¼ cup flour
1 cup milk
½ lb. sharp Cheddar
cheese, grated

½ tsp. salt
⅛ tsp. paprika
½ tsp. dry mustard
Dash cayenne
6 eggs, separated

Preheat oven to 325°F.

Melt butter. Add flour and blend. Cook over low heat 5 minutes. Do not brown. Add milk. Cook, stirring constantly, until thick and smooth. Add remaining ingredients except eggs. Beat yolks. Add equal amount of hot mixture to yolks and mix. Add egg mixture to remaining cheese mixture, mixing well. Set aside.

Beat whites until stiff but not dry. Fold cheese mixture into beaten whites. Pour into ungreased 2-quart casserole. Swirl a circle with spatula 1-inch from edge. Bake 1 hour and 15 minutes.

A decorative design may be made on top of soufflé by cutting thin slices of Swiss cheese into diamond or triangular shapes and arranging them on top before soufflé is baked.

Serves 4.

ANN SOTHERN'S

Spaetzle Casserole

SPAETZLE:

3 cups flour	4 eggs, well beaten
1 tsp. salt	½ cup water
½ tsp. baking powder	½ cup milk

Beat all ingredients together well. Drop small bits from teaspoon or through spaetzle cutter into salted simmering water. Simmer 6 to 8 minutes or until done. Remove spaetzle with slotted spoon. Plunge into cold water. Drain.

NOTE: If dumplings are heavy, add a bit more water to the batter.

CASSEROLE:

1 recipe spaetzle	2 tsps. salt
½ cup finely chopped onion	¼ tsp. white pepper
¼ cup butter	¼ lb. sliced Swiss cheese
2 cups grated sharp Cheddar cheese	

Preheat oven to 350°F.

Prepare spaetzle as directed. Sauté onion in butter until lightly browned. Set aside.

Combine spaetzle, sautéed onions, Cheddar cheese, salt and pepper. Place ½ in 2-quart casserole. Top with 2 slices Swiss cheese, remaining spaetzle and remaining Swiss cheese. Bake 30 to 35 minutes or until cheese melts and is bubbly.

Serves 6 to 8.

HAL MARCH'S
Spinach Scramble

½ lb. ground round	4 eggs, beaten
2 Tbs. minced onion	1 tsp. salt
1 Tb. olive oil	¼ tsp. pepper
½ clove garlic	
½ cup well-drained cooked spinach	

Sauté beef and onion in olive oil until golden brown. Squeeze garlic in garlic press. Add juice. *(Do not add clove.)* Add spinach; mix well. Add eggs, salt and pepper. Stir over medium heat until eggs are desired firmness

Serves 4.

JAYE P. MORGAN'S
Swiss Fondue

1 lb. Gruyère cheese	Salt and pepper to taste
1 clove garlic	Pinch grated nutmeg
1 Tb. butter	3 Tbs. kirsch (cherry liqueur)
1 Tb. flour	
½ cup milk	1 loaf French bread cut into 1-inch pieces
1 to 1½ cups dry white wine (Neuchâtel)	

Cut cheese into ¼- to ½-inch chunks.

Rub 1-quart round chafing dish, casserole, electric fry pan or saucepan with garlic. Discard. Melt butter over moderate heat. Add flour. Stir until well combined. Add milk and cook until thickened.

Gradually add cheese and wine alternately. Be certain cheese melts. Amount of wine depends upon taste.

Add seasonings and kirsch. Keep over low heat while serving.

To eat, dip bread cubes into melted cheese with long-handled fondue forks.

Serves 4 to 6.

NOTE: Be certain to use natural cheese, not processed.

Meats, Stews, and Pastas

ANN MILLER'S
Boeuf Bourguignonne

½ lb. salt pork, ¼ inch thick, cut in 1-inch squares
1 can pearl onions, drained; 1 lb.
4 lbs. beef chuck, 1½- to 2-inch cubes
1 Tb. flour
Peppercorns
2 cloves garlic, crushed

Peel of 1 orange
2 tsps. salt
4 bay leaves
1 tsp. thyme
¼ tsp. nutmeg
8 sprigs parsley
1 tsp. oregano
½ fifth burgundy
1⅓ cups mushrooms, or 8-oz. can

Brown salt pork in cast iron pot until crisp. Remove pork; reserve. Sauté onions in fat until browned. Remove onions; reserve. Dust meat with flour. Sprinkle generously with freshly ground pepper. Brown meat. Add salt pork and remaining ingredients except mushrooms and onions. Cover and cook at 250° to 300°F. for 3 hours either in oven or on top of stove. Add mushrooms (include canning liquor) and onions. Cook 15 minutes longer. Remove parsley, orange peel and bay leaves.

Serves 12.

NOTE: Keep lid on pot during cooking, said Annie when she gave us this recipe: "I do not cook too well, so whenever this recipe does not turn out too well I always throw in an old tap shoe for extra flavor. Call it my special touch!"

GENEVIEVE'S

Chili Con Carne

1 lb. ground beef
1 cup coarsely chopped
onion
½ cup coarsely
chopped green
pepper
3 Tbs. fat
3½ cups tomatoes,
or 30-oz. can
½ cup finely chopped
celery

½ cup finely chopped
carrots
2½ tsps. salt
½ tsp. paprika
Dash cayenne pepper
3 whole cloves
1 bay leaf
2 Tbs. chili powder
2½ cups red kidney beans,
or 20-oz. can

Sauté meat, onions and green pepper in fat in 3-quart saucepan until well browned. Add remaining ingredients except beans. Bring to a boil. Cover and simmer 2 hours. Add water if necessary. Skim off excess fat. Add beans. Heat thoroughly.

Serves 6 to 8.

FRANK SINATRA, JR.'S

Pepperburgers

HAPPY ULCER!

2 lbs. ground beef
½ cup finely chopped
onion
⅓ cup finely chopped
celery
2 Tbs. minced parsley
¾ cup oatmeal,
uncooked

2 tsps. salt
1½ Tbs. pepper
1 cup tomato juice
2 eggs, well beaten
1 cup tomato sauce

Preheat broiler.

Combine all ingredients except tomato sauce. Shape into eight ¾-inch thick patties. Top each with 1 tablespoon tomato sauce. Broil 4 to 6 minutes. Turn. Repeat.

Serves 8.

NOTE: Frank Junior is one of the nicest young men I've ever met. His father should be very proud of him, and he is. But, between you and me, if he were my boy I'd wash his mouth out with soap . . . and mine with a gallon of cold water . . . if he put all that pepper in any hamburger of mine! So, if your taste buds are more like mine than like Young Frank's, you'll cut down on the pepper and enjoy a burger that's really unusual. It's the oatmeal that makes it different and, come to think of it, since oatmeal is a breakfast food I think I'll try it some morning. With orange juice, of course.

GEORGE KIRBY'S

Con Carne

½ lb. ground beef
½ cup chopped onion
¼ cup diced green
　　pepper
2 cups chili without
　　beans, or 1-lb. can
2½ cups dark red
　　kidney beans,
　　or 20-oz. can

1 tsp. garlic salt
Ground red pepper to taste
4 frankfurters, sliced into
　　½-inch-thick rings
1 can tamales, about 1 lb.

Preheat oven to 350°F.

Sauté meat, onions and green pepper until meat is well browned. Add remaining ingredients except frankfurters and tamales. Simmer for ½ hour. Pour into 1½-quart casserole. Top first with frankfurters and then tamales. Bake ½ hour or until tamales are lightly browned. Serve with oyster crackers.

Serves 4.

WALTER SLEZAK'S

Fondue Bourguignonne

For four, you'll need a 1-quart fondue dish, plus a variety of sauces. Make sauces ahead and store in refrigerator. Keep cubed meat in refrigerator until 15 minutes before serving. Each guest will need 2 forks, one for cooking (fondue fork) and one for eating (dinner fork). Arrange meat and sauces so guests can cook and dip meat in sauces or relishes. If oil smokes or sputters, lower heat and add a few bread cubes to lower temperature.

2 cups vegetable oil or
   1 cup vegetable oil
   and ½ lb. (1 cup)
   butter
2 lbs. tenderloin of beef
   cut into ¾-inch
   cubes
Curry sauce
   (recipe follows)

Chutney
Diced green onions
Catsup
Barbecue sauce
Prepared hot or mild
   mustard sauce
Béarnaise sauce
   (recipe follows)
Salt, pepper, paprika

Heat oil or oil and butter in fondue dish on stove to boiling. (If butter is used, it will darken.) Transfer fondue dish to its own rack, over flame. Spear meat with fondue fork and cook in the oil to doneness desired.

Serves 4.

CURRY SAUCE:

½ cup mayonnaise
2 Tbs. milk

1 Tb. curry powder
¼ tsp. Tabasco

Combine all ingredients. Refrigerate until needed. Makes ½ cup.

BÉARNAISE SAUCE:

2 Tbs. tarragon vinegar
½ cup dry white wine
1 peppercorn
2 tsps. finely chopped
shallots
2 tsps. fresh tarragon
or ¾ tsp. dried
tarragon

2 tsps. fresh finely chopped
chervil or ¾ tsp. dried
chervil
2 egg yolks
¼ tsp. salt
⅔ cup melted butter
2 tsps. minced parsley
Dash cayenne pepper

Combine vinegar, wine, peppercorn, shallots, tarragon and chervil in saucepan; cook over low heat until reduced in half. Beat yolks and salt in top of double boiler until creamy and thick; gradually add wine mixture beating continuously to prevent curdling. Gradually add butter, beating continuously until consistency of heavy cream. Place over hot water and beat 1 minute longer. Strain sauce and add parsley and cayenne. Makes 1 cup.

CHARLIE WEAVER'S

Hamburger Gravy

½ lb. ground beef
1½ cups finely chopped
Bermuda onion
½ tsp. salt
¼ tsp. pepper
1 Tb. cumin

1 Tb. shortening
2 cups tomato sauce,
or 1-lb. can
2 cups kidney beans,
or 1-lb. can (optional)

Sauté beef and onions with seasonings in shortening over low heat in electric frying pan or skillet 15 to 20 minutes or until browned. Add tomato sauce. Cover and simmer slowly 45 minutes. Serve over spaghetti or add kidney beans and cook 15 minutes longer.

Serves 6.

CAROL BURNETT'S
Lazy Cook's Meat Loaf

½ cup milk
2 eggs
⅔ cup bread crumbs
1 Tb. garlic salt
1 tsp. pepper
½ cup finely chopped
   onion

¼ cup finely chopped
   green pepper
3 lbs. ground round
1 can tomato sauce,
   about 1 lb.

Preheat oven to 350°F.

Beat milk and eggs together in large mixing bowl. Add remaining ingredients in order given except tomato sauce. Add ½ cup tomato sauce. Combine meat mixture well. Shape into loaf. Place in greased baking pan. Pour remaining sauce over meat loaf. Bake 1¼ to 1½ hours or until done.

Serves 10 to 12.

BETSY PALMER'S
Oxtail Roman Style

4 lbs. oxtail cut into
  2-inch pieces
1 Tb. shortening
2 slices bacon, cut into
  ½-inch pieces
½ cup sliced onion
½ clove garlic, crushed
½ cup diced carrots,
  ½-inch pieces

1 tsp. chopped parsley
2 tsps. salt
½ tsp. pepper
1¼ cups dry red wine
3 Tbs. tomato paste
6 cups water
6 stalks celery, cut into
  1-inch pieces

Melt shortening and sauté oxtail, bacon and vegetables in 8-quart Dutch oven 30 minutes or until well browned, turning as necessary. Add salt, pepper and wine and cook until wine has evaporated. Combine tomato paste and water. Pour over oxtails. Cover and simmer over low heat 4 to 4½ hours or until tender. Add celery and continue cooking 15 to 20 minutes or until celery is done. Serve with noodles, rice or potatoes.

Serves 4.

MOTHER DOWD'S
Beef Pot Roast

3 to 4 lbs. blade or arm
  pot roast
2 Tbs. lard or drippings
1 cup sliced onion
½ cup seedless raisins

2 tsps. salt
½ tsp. pepper
2 bay leaves
½ cup water

Brown meat on both sides in Dutch oven or heavy skillet. Pour off fat. Add remaining ingredients. Cover and simmer 3 to 4 hours or until tender. Add more water if necessary.

Place meat on serving platter. Remove excess fat from pan drippings. Use drippings to make gravy.

Serves 6 to 8.

OZZIE AND HARRIET NELSON'S

Sherried Beef

3 lbs. stewing beef,
    cut in 1½-inch
    cubes

2 cans undiluted con-
    densed cream of
    mushroom soup,
    about 10¼ ozs. each

1 cup sherry wine
¼ cup dry onion soup mix

Preheat oven to 325°F.

Combine all ingredients in Dutch oven. Cover and bake for 3 hours. Serve with dumplings, noodles and/or carrots.

Serves 6 to 8.

MOTHER DOWD'S

Sloppy Joe Sandwich

1½ lbs. ground beef
¼ cup cooking oil
½ cup finely chopped
    onion
¼ cup finely chopped
    green pepper
14-oz. bottle catsup

¼ tsp. allspice
1 tsp. salt
½ tsp. pepper
1 tsp. dry mustard
¼ tsp. garlic powder
1 Tb. vinegar

Sauté meat in oil until lightly browned.

Add onions and peppers. Continue cooking until onions are transparent. Add remaining ingredients. Cover and simmer 1 hour stirring frequently. Skim off excess fat. Serve on hamburger buns. Serves 8.

GLORIA DE HAVEN'S

Slumgullion

1 lb. ground sirloin
2 Tbs. shortening
½ cup chopped green pepper
1 cup chopped Spanish onion
2 cans chopped mushrooms, drained, 4 ozs. each
2 cans Mexican corn, drained, 12 ozs. each

1 large can tomato sauce; about 1 lb.
¼ tsp. monosodium glutamate
2 tsps. seasoned salt
¼ tsp. Worcestershire sauce
Dash Tabasco

Melt shortening in electric frying pan. Sauté meat, green pepper, onion and mushrooms in shortening until browned. Add remaining ingredients. Cover and simmer 1 hour. Mixture should not be soupy. Serve over buttered rice or noodles.

Serves 6 to 8.

ROBERTA PETERS'

Beef Filet Piccata

8 tenderloin steaks,	1 tsp. salt
1 inch thick	⅛ tsp. pepper
2 Tbs. flour	¼ tsp. monosodium
2 Tbs. olive oil	glutamate
¾ cup beef broth	Juice of ½ lemon
1 Tb. butter	1 tsp. chopped parsley

Pound filets to ½-inch thickness. Dredge in flour. Fry for 1 minute on each side in olive oil in heavy skillet over high heat. Drain off olive oil; discard. Add remaining ingredients. Cover and simmer over low heat 5 minutes or doneness desired. Garnish with lemon slice.

Serves 4 or more.

NOTE: Not only does this lovely opera star sing in many languages, she cooks that way, too. She's been my guest, and a delightful one, on many occasions, and each time she asks if she can cook. (This is quite a rarity among guests.) She always cooks something from another land, another heritage, than her native U.S.A. And she always sings while she cooks, a wonderful combination. You'll find several of her recipes in this book but, for her voice accompaniment, you'll have to buy one of her record albums.

JIMMY NELSON'S

London Broil À La Farfel

2 round steaks	1 Tb. steak sauce
2½ inches thick	1 tsp. garlic powder
Meat tenderizer	1 Tb. dry mustard
as needed	2 drops Tabasco
½ cup tarragon vinegar	½ lemon, juiced
½ cup vegetable oil	

Apply meat tenderizer to steaks as manufacturer directs.

Combine remaining ingredients to make marinade. Marinate meat, turning frequently, for 3 to 4 hours.

Prepare hot charcoal fire on outdoor grill. When coals are white hot, grill steaks. Cook 10 minutes on each side basting with marinade. Outside will be crusty and inside pink.

Slice on bias with grain of meat into ¼-inch-thick slices. Serve with matzo farfel or whipped potatoes.

Serves 4.

BETSY PALMER'S

Pepper Steak

This favorite can be charcoal-broiled or pan-broiled in heavy iron skillet.

1½ Tbs. peppercorns or "cracked" pepper	1 tsp. salt
	¼ cup sweet butter
1 top sirloin steak, 2 inches thick	Juice of ¼ lemon
	1 Tb. chopped parsley
1 tsp. Worcestershire sauce	1 Tb. Cognac or brandy

Crush peppercorns and press into steak on both sides with heel of hand. Let steak stand 30 to 45 minutes.

Prepare medium-hot charcoal fire on outdoor grill. When coals are white hot, prepare steaks. Grill 6 to 8 minutes on first side. Season with Worcestershire sauce. Turn and grill 6 to 8 minutes or to desired doneness. Remove to a hot platter. Sprinkle with salt. Top with butter, lemon juice and parsley. Flame with brandy, slice and serve with butter sauce drippings.

Or, heat iron skillet hot. Add salt and cook stirring constantly until lightly browned. Pan-fry steak 6 to 8 minutes on each side or to desired doneness. Remove to a hot platter. Add Worcestershire sauce and butter to pan. Cook only until hot. Pour over steak. Top with lemon juice and parsley. Flame with brandy before serving. Slice and serve with butter sauce from pan.

Serves 2.

MARY AND VINCENT PRICE'S

Pepper Steak

3 cloves garlic, minced	1 Tb. oil
1 Tb. olive oil	1 Tb. butter
½ tsp. meat tenderizer	1 cup dry white wine
1 Tb. ground pepper	¼ cup butter
1 steak (approximately 2 lbs.), 1 inch thick	½ tsp. salt

Allow ½ pound steak per serving. Combine garlic, oil, tenderizer and pepper. Rub mixture into both sides of steak. Marinate 2 to 3 hours at room temperature or overnight in refrigerator.

When ready to cook, heat heavy iron skillet hot. Add oil and butter. Pan-fry steak 5 minutes on each side for a rare steak; 7 for medium and 9 for well done. Remove to heated serving platter. Add wine to skillet and bring to a boil. Add butter and salt. Serve over steak.

Serves 4.

NOTE: This is a variation of the Whitehall Club recipe that Mary and Vincent included in their book *A Treasury of Great Recipes*.

*Here I am, in the safety of my home, whipping up
a Caesar Douglas Salad as my wife Gen gives me a taste*

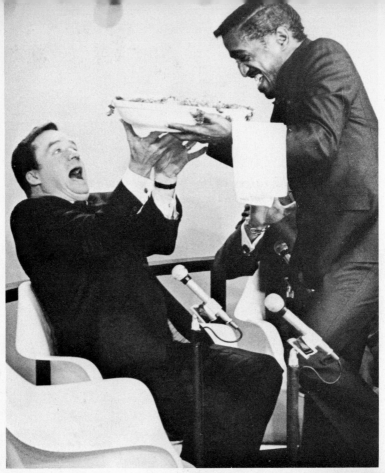

*Sammy Davis Jr. tries to give me
slightly more than a taste
of his salad—right in my lap*

*Barbara Rush convinces me
that a bird in the bath
is worth two in the pot
so I apply the back brush*

Carol Channing whips up a cookie batter.
Me? I'm being allegedly helpful

Carol Lawrence is the cook,
Martha Raye, Gig Young, and I are the kibitzers

Martha Raye and I measure bites,
but she wins by a mouthful

It takes cloak-and-dagger tactics
to get a Vincent Price recipe away from him

That's not Granny Cook,
it is Louis Nye come to apply for the job

*Carol Burnett reacts
when her recipe takes
an unexpected turn*

*One of the nicest guests
I've ever had
is Muriel Humphrey*

How did George Kirby's recipe turn out?
Just right

Betsy Palmer's recipe is great—
however you eat it

Lady Bird Johnson is wonderful,
and so is her pecan pie

E PUDDIN

When Roberta Peters cooked,
THE MIKE DOUGLAS SHOW
hit a high note

*I try to get things stirring
for Nancy Wilson*

Connie Francis laughs (I wonder why?)
when her mother tries to make me an Italian cook

When I take over
the cooking chores,
sometimes it's enough
to make a beautiful
woman cry; in this case,
it is Rene Carpenter

*I try to teach Bennett Cerf how to open an egg—one-handed—
and he promises to look it up in his Funk & Wagnalls*

*Anna Moffo introduces me to a delicacy whose name I can't pronounce,
but I'm enjoying every mouthful of the fine recipe, which is on page 141*

I help Minnie Pearl bore out some corn pone
as Grandpa Jones looks on with disgust—
or is that just plain resignation . . . or frustration?

Trini Lopez can't hide his delight
when his former teacher, Mrs. Mary Haines, of Dallas,
presents him with a box of the same homemade cookies
that helped keep him from becoming a high-school dropout

All reports to the contrary,
Al Martino and I are not whipping up a cake batter

*I make myself a member of Skitch Henderson's jug band
in retaliation for his Eggs Orange recipe*

One guess what the dish is
that makes Jane Morgan squeal with delight!

Joanie Sommers and I hop aboard
for a fast ride to her pierogi plant

*Morey Amsterdam tells me
how he makes fried rice . . . and that is a laugh!*

*E. G. Marshall gives Maureen Stapleton
a taste of one of his health-food
concoctions as The Lettermen, brave men,
gather round to help as and if needed*

*Gloria DeHaven's contribution to this book
is a Slum Gulion, which, you'd think, is hardly a dish
for so feminine a person. Not until you taste it, that is*

*Henny Youngman brought his fiddle
to the studio, but we made him swap it
for a Dutch oven*

*Ann Miller tries to teach me
one of her dance steps,
but I do much better digging into her Boeuf Bourguignonne
when Carol Walek serves it for lunch*

*We're obviously having a laugh—Don Rickles,
Jimmy Nelson, a four-legged friend, and me—
but not about Jimmy's cooking*

*Dan and I visit the ARA test kitchens,
where Carol Walek has lunch waiting:
Ann Miller's Boeuf Bourguignonne
and Carol's spinach salad*

The authors at work:
In goes the spoken word, out comes a book

RECIPES

JOHN PAYNE'S
Strip Steak

5 cups red onion slices,
    ⅛ inch thick
¼ lb. butter
1½ Tbs. salt
½ tsp. freshly ground
    pepper

1½ Tbs. prepared mustard
1½ Tbs. Worcestershire
    sauce
2 Tbs. red wine
1 sirloin strip
    (approximately 8 lbs.)

Prepare medium-hot charcoal fire on outdoor grill.

Place ½ of onions on 18 x 24-inch heavy aluminum foil. Dot with ½ of butter. Combine salt, pepper, mustard, Worcestershire sauce and wine. Brush meat with this seasoning mixture. Place meat on onions. Add remaining onions and butter. Top with a second sheet of foil. Wrap tightly.

When coals are white hot, cook meat 45 to 60 minutes depending upon thickness. Turn once during cooking. Remove foil and cook over direct heat on rack 8 to 9 minutes on each side. Place meat on heated platter. Top with onions.

Serves 16 to 24.

MOTHER DOWD'S
Rolled Stuffed Round Steak

3 cups fresh bread
    crumbs
¼ cup chopped onion
¼ cup chopped celery
1 Tb. minced parsley
½ tsp. sage
½ tsp. salt

¼ tsp. pepper
⅓ cup beef broth
1 round steak ½ inch thick
    (approximately 3 lbs.)
¼ cup lard or shortening
2 cups beef broth

Combine crumbs, vegetables and seasonings. Add broth. Toss lightly. Spread crumb mixture on steak. Roll up like a jelly roll. Fasten with butcher's string or skewers.

Brown meat in lard or shortening in heavy-bottomed pan. Add broth. Cover and simmer 1½ to 2 hours or until tender. Remove string or skewers. Cut crosswise into 1-inch slices. Use pan drippings for gravy if desired.

Serves 4.

NOTE: If whole round steak is not available, purchase 2 top round steaks. Place them side by side before spreading crumb mixture.

HARRIET VAN HORNE'S

Dinner Party

2 lbs. cubed beef	1 Tb. Kitchen Bouquet
3½ cups beef broth	2 tsps. salt
1 cup coarsely chopped onion	1 cup sliced mushrooms
¼ cup sherry	1 cup chopped celery, ¼-inch pieces
1 cup diced carrots, ½-inch pieces	1 cup chopped watercress
2 mint leaves	¼ cup chopped parsley
3 tomatoes, peeled and diced	⅔ cup green noodles

In covered pot cook beef and broth over low heat for 1 hour. Add onions and sherry and continue cooking 1 hour or until beef is tender. Meanwhile cook carrots and mint in water to cover 15 to 20 minutes or until almost tender. Drain.

Add remaining raw ingredients to meat. Cook 20 minutes longer. Add carrots.

Serves 6.

NOTE: The rest of what goes into newspaper columnist Harriet Van Horne's Dinner Party menu is French bread and butter, a California red wine, lemon sherbet and cookies.

BETTY HUGHES'S
Irish Beef Stew Pie

4 lbs. stewing beef,
  cut into 2-inch cubes
½ cup flour
¼ cup shortening
1 cup minced onion
2 cloves garlic, minced
1 qt. hot water
1 lemon, juiced
1 Tb. Worcestershire
  sauce
4 bay leaves
2 Tbs. salt
1 tsp. pepper

1 tsp. paprika
⅛ tsp. ground cloves
2 tsps. sugar
2 lbs. carrots, cut into
  2-inch pieces
1 lb. mushroom caps
2 cans white onions,
  drained, 8 ozs. each
4 cups white potatoes,
  drained; or 2 cans,
  1 lb. each
1 cup dry red wine
2 pkgs. piecrust mix

Preheat oven to 450°F.

Dredge meat in flour. Brown meat in shortening in large 6- to 8-quart Dutch oven. Add onions and garlic and cook until onions are transparent. Add water, lemon juice, seasonings, and sugar. Cover and cook 2 hours over low heat or until meat is tender. Add carrots and mushrooms. Cover and cook 20 minutes longer. Add drained onions, potatoes and wine. Cover and cook 10 minutes longer or until carrots are tender.

Make crust according to instructions on package. Divide stew into two 3-quart casseroles. Top with crust. Bake 30 minutes or until crust is golden brown.

Serves 16 to 20.

THE MYSTERY GUEST'S
Stuffed Cabbage

8 large cabbage leaves
1 lb. ground beef
2 eggs
½ cup finely chopped
   onion

1 clove garlic, crushed
1 tsp. salt
½ tsp. pepper
1 can sauerkraut,
   about 1 lb.

Wilt cabbage leaves by pouring boiling water over them. Cut out hard core. Set aside.

Combine remaining ingredients except sauerkraut. Place ¼ cup meat mixture on flat cabbage leaf at stem end. Fold over edges of leaf and roll. Secure with toothpick.

Put sauerkraut in 3-quart saucepan. Add cabbage rolls. Cover and cook over low heat 2 hours or until done.

Makes 8 cabbage rolls; serves 4.

NOTE: Let's be honest. We call this The Mystery Guest's Stuffed Cabbage because somehow our recipe files got fouled up so badly that we no longer know from whom this tasty concoction came.

KAYE BALLARD'S
Stuffed Cabbage

1 large head cabbage
1 cup rice
2 lbs. ground beef
2 lbs. ground veal
1 cup finely chopped
   green pepper
1 cup finely chopped
   onion
2 eggs

¾ cup tomato paste
   (6 oz. can)
1 Tb. salt
1 tsp. pepper
3½ cups tomatoes,
   or 30-oz. can
Dash Tabasco
1 clove garlic, crushed

Preheat oven to 300°F.

Remove core and outer leaves from cabbage. Cook cabbage 20 minutes in salted water or until leaves separate easily. Set aside.

Cook rice according to package instructions.

Combine meat, green pepper, onion, eggs, tomato paste, salt and pepper and cooked rice. Place ½ cup meat mixture in center of each cabbage leaf. Fold over envelope style. Secure with toothpick.

To bake: Arrange neatly in 2-inch-deep baking pan. Cook tomatoes, Tabasco and garlic 15 minutes. Pour over cabbage rolls. Bake 2 hours.

To cook on top of stove: Place cabbage rolls in large saucepan. Add tomatoes, Tabasco and garlic. Cover and cook over very low heat for 2 hours or until done. Makes 20 rolls.

MOTHER DOWD'S

Stuffed Cabbage

1 large head white cabbage	¼ tsp. monosodium glutamate
1 cup raw rice	½ tsp. salt
½ cup finely chopped onion	¼ tsp. pepper
1 lb. ground beef	1 can condensed tomato soup, 10¼ ozs.
¼ cup sour cream	1 cup onion, in ¼-inch slices
1 tsp. Worcestershire sauce	

Remove core and outer leaves from cabbage. Place in saucepan. Cover with water. Bring to a boil. Cover and simmer 20 minutes or until leaves separate easily. Set aside.

Cook rice according to manufacturer's instructions. Combine

cooked rice, onion, meat, sour cream and seasonings. Place ⅓ cup meat mixture in center of each cabbage leaf. Fold over envelope style. Secure with a toothpick.

Pour soup into 3-quart saucepan. Add 2 cans water. Mix until smooth. Add onions and then cabbage rolls. Cover and cook 1½ hours or until done.

Makes 16 cabbage rolls; serves 8.

GENEVIEVE'S
Stuffed Cabbage

1 large head white
   cabbage
½ cup vinegar
1 cup minced onion
1 clove garlic, crushed
¼ cup olive oil
1 egg, beaten
1 lb. ground beef
½ cup cooked rice
1 tsp. salt

½ tsp. pepper
½ cup tomato purée
2 cups sauerkraut,
   or 1-lb. can
1 cup sliced onions
2½ cups tomatoes,
   or 20-oz. can
1 tsp. salt
¼ tsp. pepper

Remove core and outer leaves from cabbage. Place in saucepan. Cover with water. Add vinegar. Bring to a boil. Cover and simmer 20 minutes or until leaves separate easily. Set aside.

Sauté onion and garlic in olive oil until transparent. Add egg, beef, rice, ½ tsp. salt and pepper and tomato purée. Mix until well combined. Place ⅓ cup meat mixture in center of each cabbage leaf. Fold over enevelope style. Secure with a toothpick.

Place sauerkraut in 3-quart saucepan with onions arranged on top. Place cabbage rolls on onions. Combine tomatoes and salt and pepper. Pour over cabbage rolls. Cover and cook 2 hours or until done.

Makes 12 cabbage rolls; serves 6.

MOTHER DOWD'S

Swedish Meatballs in Dill Sauce

2 Tbs. finely minced
   onion
1 Tb. butter
¼ cup milk
1 egg, beaten
½ cup cracker crumbs
1 tsp. salt
½ tsp. pepper
¼ tsp. nutmeg
1 lb. ground beef
¼ lb. ground pork

¼ lb. ground veal
⅓ cup butter or margarine
¼ cup butter
¼ cup flour
2 cups beef broth
½ cup light cream
1 tsp. fresh dill or ¼ tsp.
   dried dill
½ tsp. salt
¼ tsp. white pepper

Sauté onion in 1 Tb. butter until transparent. Set aside. Combine milk and egg. Add cracker crumbs and seasonings. Set aside until crumbs absorb liquid. Add meat and onions. Mix gently but well. Shape into 1-inch balls. Sauté in ⅓ cup butter until well browned, turning as necessary. Remove meatballs from pan. Discard drippings. Prepare sauce in same pan.

Melt ¼ cup butter. Add flour stirring constantly. Cook 10 minutes over low heat stirring occasionally. Add remaining ingredients. Stir until thickened. Add meatballs and simmer 10 minutes turning several times. Serve with buttered egg noodles.
Serves 8.

MRS. SCOTT CARPENTER'S

Taco Pie

1 package corn chips,
   11 ozs. size
4 cups chili without
   beans, or 2 cans,
   1 lb. each

8 ozs. sliced mozzarella
   cheese
2 cans French fried onion
   rings, about 4 ozs. each

Preheat oven to 400°F.

Place half of corn chips in greased 2-quart casserole. Top with one can of chili, half of cheese and one can of onion rings. Repeat. Bake 30 minutes or until hot.

Serves 8.

SOUPY SALES'S

Liver Soupy

1 lb. calves liver,
    ¼ inch thick
¼ cup olive oil
2 green peppers, cut
    into ¼-inch strips
1 cup onion slices,
    ⅛ inch thick, separated into rings

¼ tsp. thyme
½ tsp. salt
¼ tsp. pepper
¼ cup white wine

Remove membrane from liver. Cut into 1-inch squares. Sauté in olive oil in frying pan 3 to 4 minutes on each side. Remove to a heated serving platter.

In same pan, sauté peppers until tender; add onions and seasonings and continue cooking until lightly browned, stirring frequently. Add wine. Stir to combine. Top liver with peppers and onions.

Serves 4.

NOTE: No pun intended (not much), but this recipe rang up a lot of soupy sales after he showed how to make it in his own inimitable style. Never did I know that so many people like liver.

Veal Chops À La Frank Parker

4 veal chops, (approximately 2 lbs.), ¾ inch thick
2 Tbs. olive oil
2 Tbs. butter
¼ tsp. rosemary

¼ tsp. oregano
½ tsp. garlic salt
½ tsp. onion salt
¼ tsp. pepper
¼ cup Marsala wine

Brown chops slowly in olive oil and butter (10 to 15 minutes each side). Add remaining ingredients. Cover and cook 15 minutes longer or until tender.

Serves 4.

AL MARTINO'S

Breaded Veal Cutlets

4 veal round steaks (cutlets), ¼ lb. each, ¼ inch thick
1 cup bread crumbs
½ tsp. salt
¼ tsp. paprika

2 eggs, beaten
¼ cup water
¼ cup olive oil
4 lemon slices
Watercress

Pound veal to flatten to ⅛-inch thickness. Dredge with bread crumbs which have been seasoned with salt and paprika; shake off excess. Combine egg and water. Dip meat in egg mixture; drain. Dredge again with bread crumbs.

Sauté quickly over high heat in olive oil (approximately 5 minutes on each side). Serve with lemon slices and watercress garnish.

Serves 4.

ANITA BRYANT'S

Anita Birds

8 veal round steaks
  (cutlets), ¼ inch
  thick
8 slices boiled ham
8 slices processed Swiss
  cheese
¼ cup flour
1 egg, beaten

2 Tbs. water
1 cup Corn Flakes crumbs
1 can condensed cream of
  mushroom soup,
  about 10¼ ozs.
1 cup light cream
¼ cup sauterne

Preheat oven to 350°F.

Pound veal to flatten to ⅛-inch thickness. Top each slice first with ham. Cut each slice of cheese into 4 strips and stack on ham. Roll meat loosely around cheese. Secure with toothpicks. Dredge veal birds in flour. Combine egg and water. Dip veal birds in egg mixture; drain. Coat with crumbs. Place seam side down in 13 x 9 x 1½-inch baking dish.

In saucepan combine remaining ingredients. Bring to a boil. Pour around veal birds. Cover pan and bake 50 minutes or until tender. Uncover and continue to bake 10 minutes or until crumbs are crisp.

Makes 8 birds.

MOTHER DOWD'S

Veal Cutlet Cordon Bleu

4 veal round steaks
  (cutlets), ¼ inch
  thick
4 slices prosciutto ham
4 slices natural Swiss
  cheese
3 Tbs. flour

1 egg, slightly beaten
¼ cup milk
½ cup bread crumbs
½ tsp. salt
⅛ tsp. pepper
¼ cup olive oil or butter

Pound veal to flatten to ⅛-inch thickness. Top each slice first with ham and then cheese. Be certain that ham and cheese are ½ inch smaller in diameter than veal. Fold in half. Pound edges of veal together. Dredge with flour. Combine eggs and milk. Dip veal in egg mixture; drain. Coat with seasoned crumbs. Sauté over high heat in oil until brown (10 minutes).

Serves 4.

RANDOLPH JONES'S
Veal Chip Delight

6 veal round steaks
  (cutlets), ¼ inch
  thick
6 slices proscuitto ham
6 slices natural Swiss
  cheese
¼ cup flour
1 egg, slightly beaten
¼ cup milk
1 cup crushed potato
  chips

1 cup butter or margarine
1 cup crushed potato chips
1 tsp. instant minced onion
½ tsp. monosodium
  glutamate
¼ tsp. white pepper
1 pt. sour cream
2 Tbs. minced chives

Pound veal to flatten to ⅛-inch thickness. Top each slice first with ham and then cheese. Roll meat, tuck in sides, and press ends to seal. Dredge each portion in flour. Combine egg and milk. Dip veal rolls in egg mixture; drain. Coat with potato chip crumbs. Heat ½ cup butter or margarine in heavy skillet. Sauté veal rolls until golden brown, 5 to 7 minutes on each side.

Melt ½ cup butter or margarine in heavy-bottomed saucepan or skillet. Carefully stir in potato chips and seasonings. Cook over low heat for 5 minutes. Add sour cream and cook 10 minutes longer, stirring frequently. Place veal rolls on warm platter. Spoon sauce over rolls. Garnish with minced chives.

Serves 6.

GENEVIEVE'S

Veal Scallopini

1½ lbs. veal round
   steaks (cutlets),
   ¼ inch thick
¾ tsp. salt
½ cup flour
¼ cup butter
¼ cup oil

1 cup sliced fresh mush-
   rooms, ¼ inch thick
1 chicken bouillon cube
3 Tbs. water
½ lemon
Freshly ground pepper
Toast points

Remove tough membrane from veal. Season with salt; sprinkle with flour. Flatten, turning once, to ⅛-inch thickness.

Sauté veal in hot butter and oil in heavy skillet until browned; turn. Remove veal to heated serving platter. Add mushrooms to skillet, cover and cook 3 to 4 minutes, stirring several times. Add bouillon cube and water; bring to a boil. Pour pan gravy around veal. Using fork, twist juice from lemon over veal. Sprinkle with freshly ground pepper. Serve with toast points.

Serves 4.

ANNE BAXTER'S

Lamb Kidneys

1 lb. lamb kidneys
1 cup milk
6 Tbs. butter
1 Tb. Dijon mustard
1 tsp. salt

¼ tsp. white pepper
Few leaves fresh tarragon
½ cup heavy cream
1 Tb. chopped parsley

Split kidneys and remove white membrane and cord. Soak in milk for 10 minutes, drain and dry. Cut into thin slices. Sauté in butter for 5 minutes over low heat. Add mustard, seasonings and cream. Simmer 2 minutes longer. Serve on toast tips or buttered rice. Garnish with chopped parsley.

Serves 4.

MOTHER DOWD'S

Irish Stew

4 cups diced roast lamb,
½-inch pieces
1½ cups sliced onion,
⅛ inch thick
1 cup diced carrots,
½-inch pieces
½ cup celery crescents,
¼ inch thick
2 cups diced potatoes,
½-inch pieces

1 cup diced turnip,
½-inch pieces
¼ cup chopped parsley
1 tsp. salt
¼ tsp. pepper
4 cups beef broth
2 Tbs. lamb fat, melted
2 Tbs. flour

Place all ingredients except lamb fat and flour in 4-quart saucepan. Bring to a boil. Simmer 20 minutes or until vegetables are almost tender. Make paste from lamb fat and flour. Add to stew. Mix until dissolved. Continue cooking 10 minutes.

Serves 8.

WALTER JETTON'S
(LBJ'S BBQ CHEF)

Barbecue Sauce

1 cup catsup
½ cup cider vinegar
¼ cup Worcestershire
sauce
½ cup water
1 tsp. sugar
1 tsp. paprika
1 tsp. chili powder

1 tsp. salt
¼ tsp. black pepper
3 bay leaves
1 clove garlic
3 stalks celery, chopped
2 Tbs. chopped onions
¼ cup butter

Combine all ingredients in a saucepan and bring to a boil. Simmer 15 minutes. Remove from heat and strain. Serve hot with beef, chicken or spareribs.

TO BARBECUE SPARERIBS:

4 lbs. spareribs   2 lemons,
2 tsps. salt   sliced 1/8 inch thick
1/2 tsp. pepper

Preheat oven to 450°F.

Spread spareribs, meaty side up, in shallow baking pan. Sprinkle with salt and pepper. Spread lemon slices on top. Bake for 30 minutes uncovered. Pour sauce over meat. Reduce oven temperature to 350°F. Bake 1 hour longer basting occasionally.

Serves 4 to 6.

MOTHER DOWD'S

Dutch Kale and Smoked Sausage

1 lb. kale   Water to cover
2 lbs. smoked sausage   2 tsps. salt
12 medium-sized pota-   1/4 lb. butter
    toes, pared and   2 tsps. salt
    quartered   1/2 tsp. pepper

Wash and stem kale. Steam in water that clings to leaves in covered 8-quart saucepan just until wilted (15 to 20 minutes). Drain. Chop. Set aside.

Meanwhile simmer sausage in water to cover 20 minutes.

Cook potatoes in salted boiling water until tender (20 to 25 minutes). Drain. Mash, add butter, salt and pepper. Whip until light and fluffy. Add chopped kale. Mix to blend. Serve with sausage.

Serves 8.

MOREY AMSTERDAM'S

Fried Rice

¼ lb. diced pork or
    shrimp (peeled and
    deveined, cut into
    ½-inch pieces)
2 Tbs. chopped onion

3 Tbs. oil
3 cups cooked rice
1 Tb. soy sauce
2 eggs, scrambled
¼ cup chives

Cook pork or shrimp and onions in oil in heavy-bottomed pan until meat is well done. Add remaining ingredients. Toss lightly.
Serves 6.

MOTHER DOWD'S

Ham Loaf

2 lbs. ham
1 lb. fresh pork
    shoulder
1 cup milk
1 egg, beaten

1 cup bread crumbs
¼ tsp. pepper
⅛ tsp. nutmeg
⅛ tsp. poultry seasoning

Preheat oven to 350°F.

Have butcher grind ham and pork together. Combine milk and egg. Add crumbs and seasonings. Set aside until all moisture is absorbed. Add meat. Mix until well combined. Shape into loaf. Bake in shallow baking dish 1½ hours or until internal temperature reaches 165 to 175°F.

Serves 12.

MOTHER DOWD'S

Sauerkraut Viennese

2 lbs. link sausage
3½ cups sauerkraut,
   or 20-oz. can
1 cup water

3 whole cloves
1 bay leaf
½ tsp. salt
1 cup sour cream

Preheat oven to 350°F.

Bake sausage in shallow pan until well browned (about 45 minutes).

Meanwhile, boil rapidly sauerkraut, water and seasonings in saucepan until liquid has evaporated. Remove cloves and bay leaf. Add sour cream. Continue cooking until hot, stirring constantly. Place sauerkraut on platter. Top with baked sausage.

Serves 6.

ANNIE FARGE'S

Chou Blanch Au Saucisse (Cabbage and Sausage)

2 lbs. link sausage
3 cups sliced cooked
   potatoes (approxi-
   mately 6 to 7 me-
   dium-sized potatoes)
6 cups shredded cab-
   bage (approxi-
   mately 1½ lbs.
   as purchased)

½ cup water
2 tsps. salt
¼ tsp. pepper

In electric skillet (325°F.) cook sausage until golden brown (15 minutes), turning as necessary. Drain grease. Add potatoes, cabbage, water, salt and pepper. Reduce heat to 220°F., cover and cook ½ hour.

Serves 6.

MOTHER DOWD'S

Bohemian Spareribs

2 lbs. spareribs, cut
crosswise in half
1 tsp. salt
½ tsp. pepper
2½ cups sauerkraut,
or 20-oz. can

1 Tb. caraway seeds
½ cup sliced onions,
⅛ inch thick, separated
into rings
2½ cups tomatoes, crushed;
or 20-oz. can

Preheat oven to 350°F.

Cut spareribs into 1-rib portions. Season with salt and pepper. Set aside. Mix sauerkraut and caraway seeds. Place sauerkraut in greased 9 x 14-inch baking dish. Top with onion rings, crushed tomatoes and spareribs. Bake 2 hours.

Serves 4.

ZSA ZSA GABOR'S

Szekely Gulyas

2 lbs. fresh pork butt,
diced ½ inch thick
1 cup finely chopped
onion
2 tsps. paprika
2 tsps. salt
1 tsp. caraway seeds

½ tsp. pepper
¼ cup shortening
2 cans sauerkraut,
about 1 lb. each
2 lbs. link sausage,
cut into 1-inch pieces
1 cup sour cream

Sauté pork, onions and seasonings in shortening in Dutch oven until well browned. Cover and cook over low heat 1 hour, stirring occasionally. Add sauerkraut and sausage. Mix to combine. Cover and continue cooking ½ hour longer. Skim off excess fat. Garnish with sour cream.

Serves 12 to 14.

CAROL WALEK'S

Mexican Sombrero Sandwich

This original recipe was one of the top twenty in the 1967 National Sandwich Idea Contest.

6 Tbs. salad dressing	1 cup minced cooked ham
¾ cup chopped stuffed green olives	(¼ lb.)
	12 slices white bread
1 cup shredded Cheddar cheese	2 eggs
	½ cup milk
Dash chili powder	1 cup Corn Flakes crumbs
10 drops Tabasco sauce	

Preheat deep fat fryer to 375°F.

Combine salad dressing, olives, cheese, chili powder, Tabasco sauce and ham. Mix well. Spread ¼ cup on each of six bread slices. Top with remaining bread.

Beat eggs; blend in milk. Coat sandwich with egg mixture. Dredge with Corn Flakes crumbs. Deep-fry 1 minute or until golden brown. Serve immediately.

Serves 6.

MOTHER DOWD'S

Macaroni and Meat—Country Style

2 cups elbow macaroni (8-oz. pkg.)	2½ cups kidney beans, or 20-oz. can
1¼ lbs. ground beef	1 cup cooked peas
1 cup sliced onion	2½ tsps. salt
1 clove garlic, minced	½ tsp. pepper
2 pimientos, chopped	

Cook macaroni according to instructions on package. Drain. Set aside until needed.

Sauté meat in 4-quart saucepan until lightly browned. Add onions and garlic. Continue cooking until onions are transparent. Add macaroni and remaining ingredients. Cook until thoroughly heated.

Serves 8 to 10.

NOTE: Mixture may be prepared ahead, stored in greased 3-quart casserole in refrigerator, and heated for 1¼ hours in 350°F. oven.

DENNIS O'KEEFE'S

Special Macaroni Casserole

1 package elbow macaroni (16 ozs.)	½ cup melted butter
1 cup finely chopped onion	1 lb. American cheese, grated
2 lbs. ground beef	2 cans cream of tomato soup, undiluted,
1 tsp. salt	10¼ ozs. each
½ tsp. pepper	⅔ cup water

Preheat oven to 350°F.

Cook macaroni according to package instructions. Meanwhile sauté onion, meat, salt and pepper in butter over moderate heat, stirring frequently, 10 minutes or until meat is browned.

Toss all ingredients together until well combined. Pour into well-greased 4-quart casserole. Bake 45 minutes or until cheese is melted and soup bubbly.

Serves 12.

JUNE VALLI'S
Special Manicotti

SAUCE:

1 cup finely chopped
   onion
1 clove garlic, minced
½ lb. ground beef
½ lb. ground veal
½ lb. bulk sweet
   sausage
2 Tbs. olive oil
3½ cups tomatoes,
   crushed, or 30-oz.
   can

⅓ cup tomato paste
1 can chopped mushrooms,
   8 ozs.
½ cup finely chopped
   celery
1 tsp. sweet basil
1 tsp. salt
½ tsp. pepper
1 tsp. sugar

Sauté onion, garlic and meat in olive oil, stirring frequently, in heavy-bottomed saucepan, 15 minutes or until well browned. Add remaining ingredients. Cover and simmer slowly 3 to 3½ hours.

MANICOTTI FILLING:

2 eggs, slightly beaten
2 lbs. ricotta cheese
½ lb. mozzarella cheese,
   diced
1 cup grated Parmesan
   cheese

½ tsp. pepper
1 tsp. salt
16 manicotti noodles,
   cooked
½ cup grated Parmesan
   cheese

Make filling by mixing first 6 ingredients. Blend thoroughly. Stuff manicotti with filling.

Preheat oven to 350°F.

Spread ⅓ sauce in bottom of shallow baking dish. Place manicotti on top. Cover with remaining sauce. Top with Parmesan. Bake 20 minutes or until sauce is bubbly.

Serves 6 to 8.

MARGE CHAMPION'S

Slops

1 package medium egg
  noodles (8 ozs.)
3 Tbs. olive oil
1½ cups minced onion
2 lbs. ground beef
½ tsp. salt
1 tsp. garlic salt
¼ tsp. pepper

2½ cups tomatoes, crushed,
  or 20-oz. can
2 cups creamed corn,
  or 1-lb. can
½ cup chopped black
  olives
1 cup grated American or
  Parmesan cheese

Preheat oven to 375°F.

Cook noodles according to package instructions *al dente*. Drain. Heat oil. Sauté onions, beef and seasonings in oil until done but not browned. Combine drained noodles, meat mixture and remaining ingredients. Pour into greased 4-quart baking dish. Bake 45 minutes or until bubbly.

Serves 12.

MOTHER DOWD'S

Tallerino

4 cups egg noodles
  (8 ozs.)
1 lb. ground round
½ cup chopped onion
½ cup chopped green
  pepper (optional)
3 Tbs. bacon fat
2 cups stewed tomatoes,
  or 1-lb. can

1 can cream style corn,
  8 ozs.
2 tsps. salt
1 Tb. chili powder
½ cup grated American
  cheese

Preheat oven to 350°F.

Cook noodles according to instructions on package. Drain. Set aside until needed.

Sauté meat, onions and green pepper in bacon fat until meat is browned. Add remaining ingredients and cooked noodles. Pour into greased 2-quart casserole. Top with cheese. Bake for 45 minutes or until thoroughly heated.

Serves 6 to 8.

NOTE: If prepared ahead of time and refrigerated, baking time will be approximately 1½ hours.

CAROL LAWRENCE'S
Mother's Ravioli *

3 cups sifted flour	1 lb. ricotta cheese
¾ tsp. salt	1 tsp. salt
3 eggs, slightly beaten	½ tsp. pepper
½ cup plus 1 Tb. lukewarm water	½ cup finely chopped parsley
½ lb. ground beef	3 egg yolks
1 Tb. olive oil	

Preheat oven to 375°F.

Sift flour and salt together into mixing bowl. Add eggs and stir with fork until well mixed. Gradually add water and stir until mixture forms a smooth ball (dough should clean the bowl but not be sticky). Turn out dough onto very lightly floured board and knead for a few minutes or until smooth and elastic. Set aside in floured covered bowl for 30 minutes.

Meanwhile, saute meat in olive oil until lightly browned. Drain excess fat. Add remaining ingredients. Mix until well blended. Cool filling.

* Thank you, Carol Lawrence's mother, for helping to make *The Mike Douglas Show* what it is.

Roll out ½ dough on lightly floured board to a 16-inch square. Put teaspoonfuls of filling about 2 inches apart on dough. Roll out remaining dough and brush with water. Put dough, moistened side down, over filling. Press edges of dough firmly around each teaspoonful of filling. With knife or pastry cutter, cut ravioli into 2-inch squares. Set aside to dry 2 hours on floured pan. Drop ravioli into boiling salted water and cook 15 minutes or until tender. Place in shallow casserole and cover with hot spaghetti sauce. Bake 25 minutes or until sauce is bubbly. Garnish with grated cheese. Serves 8.

KAYE BALLARD'S
Spaghetti and Meatballs

SAUCE:

2 chicken legs,
   cut in half
½ lb. diced beef,
   ½-inch pieces
½ lb. diced pork,
   ½-inch pieces
¼ cup oil
½ cup chopped onion
½ cup sliced
   mushrooms

½ cup Italian red wine
3½ cups tomatoes,
   or 30-oz. can
3½ cups tomato purée,
   or 30-oz. can
2 tsps. salt
½ tsp. pepper
1 Tb. oregano
1 Tb. sweet basil

Brown chicken and meat in oil over low heat 20 to 30 minutes, stirring frequently. Add onions and mushrooms and continue to cook 10 minutes stirring occasionally or until browned. Add remaining ingredients. Cover and cook over low heat 2½ hours. Meanwhile prepare meatballs as follows:

MEATBALLS:

1 lb. ground round	¼ cup milk
¼ cup grated Locatelli romano cheese	¾ cup bread crumbs
2 eggs, beaten	½ tsp. salt
¼ cup chopped parsley	½ tsp. garlic salt
1 Tb. minced onion	¼ tsp. pepper

Combine all ingredients. Shape into ¾-inch meatballs. Sauté over low heat until well browned, turning as necessary (approximately 15 minutes).

Add meatballs to sauce. Serve over spaghetti.

Serves 8 to 10.

DELLA REESE'S

Spaghetti Sauce

3 lbs. ground beef	2 cans tomato sauce, 8 ozs. each
1 clove garlic, minced	2 cans tomato paste, 6 ozs. each
2 cups chopped onion	
1 cup chopped green pepper	¾ cup water
1 bay leaf	⅓ cup pimiento-stuffed olives, chopped
2 tsps. salt	
1 tsp. monsodium glutamate	½ cup chopped pimientos
½ tsp. pepper	1 lb. spaghetti

In heavy-bottomed saucepan over moderate heat, sauté beef 15 minutes until lightly browned. Add vegetables and seasonings and continue cooking 15 minutes or until well browned. Add tomato sauce and paste and water. Cook 45 minutes. Add olives and pimientos.

Cook spaghetti as package directs. Serve sauce over spaghetti. Serves 8.

NANCY WILSON'S

Spaghetti

2 cups chopped green
  pepper
4 cups chopped onion
4 cloves garlic, minced
3½ cups tomato sauce,
  or 30-oz. can
3½ cups tomato purée,
  or 30-oz. can

3½ cups tomatoes,
  or 30-oz. can
3 Tbs. Italian seasoning
1 cup olive oil
2 lbs. ground sirloin
1 lb. spaghetti

Combine vegetables, tomatoes, seasonings and oil in 4-quart heavy-bottomed pot. Cover and simmer slowly for 8 hours. Sauté meat separately.

Cook spaghetti according to package instruction. Combine with sauce and meat.

Serves 10.

Poultry

JIMMY DURANTE'S

*Boiled Chicken with Vegetables**

1 stewing chicken, 3 to 4 lbs.	1 bay leaf
2 cups carrot rings, ¼-inch slices	1 sprig parsley
	1 Tb. salt
2 cups onion slices, ⅛-inch slices	½ tsp. pepper
	Water to cover
1 cup celery crescents, ¼-inch slices	

Wash and dry chicken; truss with legs folded back. Place chicken, vegetables and seasonings in 3-quart saucepan with water to cover. Bring to a boil. Cover and simmer slowly for 1 hour or until chicken is tender. Place chicken on heated serving platter. Garnish with the vegetables.

Serves 6.

NOTE: Strain broth and reserve for soup. Add ½ cup rice and cook until rice is tender (25 minutes).

* Jimmy's schnozzola kept getting in the way when he prepared this recipe on *The Mike Douglas Show*, but Carol Walek had no such problem in the testing.

ENZO STUARTI'S

Chicken, Castelli Romani Style

3 chicken breasts,
　1 lb. each
2 tsps. salt
¼ tsp. freshly ground
　black pepper
2 slices bacon, diced
　into ½-inch pieces

2 Tbs. butter
2 Tbs. olive oil
1 clove garlic, minced
1 Tb. tomato paste
½ cup chicken broth
½ cup white wine

Wash, dry and bone chicken. Rub with salt and pepper. Set aside.

In Dutch oven or heavy frying pan, cook bacon until crisp. Drain fat and discard. Add butter and oil. Sauté chicken and garlic until chicken is well browned, turning as necessary. Combine tomato paste, broth and wine. Add to chicken. Cover and simmer slowly 45 minutes or until chicken is tender.

Serves 3 to 4.

GIZELLE McKENZIE'S

Champagne Chicken

4 lbs. chicken parts
¼ cup flour
2 tsps. salt
¼ tsp. pepper
½ tsp. tarragon
1 Tb. chives

1 Tb. minced parsley
½ cup butter
1 cup chicken broth
Split of domestic cham-
　pagne (about 6 ozs.)

Wash and dry chicken. Dredge in flour which has been seasoned with salt and pepper. Sauté chicken and seasonings in butter in heavy skillet or Dutch oven, until golden brown on all sides. Add broth. Cover and simmer slowly 20 to 30 minutes or until chicken is tender. Add champagne. Cover and continue to cook 15 minutes.

Serves 8.

VIC DAMONE'S
Chicken À La Vic Damone

2 lbs. chicken parts
¼ cup flour
¼ cup minced onion
¼ cup finely chopped
  green pepper
¼ tsp. garlic powder

¼ tsp. pepper
2 tsps. salt
½ cup olive oil
3½ cups tomato sauce,
  or 30-oz. can

Wash and dry chicken. Dredge with flour. Sauté chicken, vegetables and seasonings in olive oil until golden on all sides. Drain off oil. Add tomato sauce. Cover and simmer slowly 45 minutes or until chicken is tender.

Serves 4.

ZSA ZSA GABOR'S
Chicken Paprikas with Egg Dumplings

1 frying chicken,
  2½ lbs.
1 tsp. salt
¼ cup butter
½ cup chopped onion
2 tsps. paprika

¼ tsp. pepper
1 cup water
2 Tbs. melted butter
2 Tbs. flour
½ pt. sour cream

Cut chicken into pieces. Wash and dry. Season with salt. Melt butter in heavy-bottomed skillet. Sauté chicken, onions, paprika and pepper until chicken is golden brown. Add water. Cover and simmer 35 minutes or until chicken is tender.

Combine melted butter and flour. Add to chicken, stirring vigorously. Continue to cook for 10 minutes over low heat. Add sour cream. Mix. Remove from heat. Serve with egg dumplings, next page.

Serves 4.

EGG DUMPLINGS

2 eggs	1 cup flour
½ tsp. salt	1 qt. water
½ tsp. melted butter	1 tsp. salt
½ cup water	

Beat eggs, salt, butter and water together. Add egg mixture gradually to flour. Stir until smooth and glossy.

Drop by teaspoonfuls into boiling salted water. Cook 5 minutes. Remove with slotted spoon.

Serves 4.

MOTHER DOWD'S

Golden Baked Chicken

2 lbs. chicken parts	¼ cup melted butter
¼ cup flour	1 can undiluted cream of
½ tsp. paprika	chicken soup, 10¼ ozs.
½ tsp. salt	½ cup water
⅛ tsp. pepper	1 Tb. minced parsley

Preheat oven to 375°F.

Wash and dry chicken. Dredge chicken in flour and seasonings. Pour melted butter in shallow baking dish. Arrange chicken in a single layer, skin side down, in baking dish. Bake 20 minutes. Turn chicken. Bake 20 minutes longer.

Blend soup and water. Pour over chicken. Sprinkle top with parsley. Bake 20 minutes longer.

Serves 6.

ROBERTA PETERS'

Jamaican Chicken

2 frying chickens,
  quartered, 2½ lbs.
  each
½ cup melted butter
½ tsp. pepper
1 Tb. seasoned salt

2 cups white seedless
  grapes, or 1-lb. can
¼ cup sugar
1 Tb. cornstarch
¼ cup Jamaica rum
½ tsp. salt

Wash and dry chicken. Brush chicken with melted butter and rub with seasonings. Set aside in refrigerator 2 to 3 hours.

Preheat broiler. Place chicken, skin side down, on rack. Broil chicken about 4 inches from heat 50 to 60 minutes under medium heat, turning 3 or 4 times and basting often. Degrease pan with ¼ cup water. Strain and save drippings. Place chicken on heated serving platter.

In saucepan combine remaining ingredients; heat *(do not boil)*. Add pan drippings. Pour sauce over chicken and serve.

Serves 8.

AUNT ELLIE VALLEE'S

Lemon Fricken Chickasee

2 frying chickens, quartered, 2½ lbs. each	2 cups sliced onion, ⅛-inch slices
12 lemons	1 Tb. oregano
1 cup olive oil	1 tsp. paprika
½ cup wine vinegar	1 Tb. salt
½ cup chopped parsley	½ tsp. pepper

Wash and dry chicken. Wash lemons. Squeeze lemons. Save skins. Combine lemon juice and remaining ingredients for marinade. Rub chicken with lemon skins. Marinate chicken 12 to 24 hours (include lemon skins in marinade).

Preheat oven to 375°F.

Remove chicken from refrigerator ½ hour before baking. Turn several times in marinade. Place chicken, skin side down, on greased baking dish. Bake for 30 minutes. Turn, baste with marinade. Bake 30 minutes longer, basting several times, or until chicken is tender.

Serves 8.

NOTE: We can thank Rudy Vallee for Auntie Ellie's recipe. But we don't know if he or she got the name of it slightly twisted. We do know though that it tastes oodgay.

IDA LUPINO'S

Quartered Chicken

1 frying chicken,
  quartered, 2½ lbs.
2 cups water
1½ tsps. salt
¼ tsp. white pepper
¼ tsp. thyme
1 bay leaf
1 package dry chicken
  noodle soup mix
2 medium-sized carrots,
  cut into 2-inch
  pieces

1 stalk celery, cut into
  1-inch pieces
¼ cup green onion,
  ¼-inch slices
1 can white potatoes,
  drained, 1 lb.
2 Tbs. flour
2 Tbs. capers

Wash chicken. Place chicken with cold water to cover in 3-quart saucepan. Bring to a boil. Drain and discard water. Add measured water, seasonings, soup mix and vegetables except potatoes. Bring to a boil. Cover and simmer slowly for 45 minutes. Add potatoes and cook 10 minutes longer. Remove chicken and vegetables to heated serving platter. Strain and reserve broth.

Skim fat from broth. Set aside 2½ tablespoons of fat and 1 cup broth for sauce. To make sauce, heat chicken fat in heavy-bottomed 1-quart suacepan. Add flour. Cook over very low heat 10 minutes. Add broth stirring vigorously. Cook 5 minutes longer. Add capers. Pour over chicken.

Serves 4.

SADIE AND HENNY YOUNGMAN'S

Chicken

1 roasting chicken,
    5 lbs.
1 Tb. salt
½ tsp. pepper
¼ tsp. garlic powder
½ tsp. paprika
2 cups chopped onions
½ cup oil

2 Tbs. pickling spices tied
    in cheesecloth
6 medium-sized potatoes,
    peeled and quartered
4 medium-sized carrots,
    cut into 2-inch pieces
1 qt. hot water

Preheat oven to 400°F.

Wash and dry chicken. Combine seasonings. Rub on inside and outside of chicken. Set aside.

In roasting pan or Dutch oven sauté onions in oil until lightly browned. Remove from heat. Place chicken, pickling spice, potatoes and carrots in pan. Add water. Cover and bake 1 hour. Remove cover. Roast 1½ to 1¾ hours longer, basting occasionally, until chicken is browned and tender. Remove pickling spices. Place chicken with vegetables surrounding it on heated serving platter.

Serves 8.

BARBARA RUSH'S

Rock Cornish Game Hens

6 Rock Cornish hens,
    1½ lbs. each
3 cups cubed white
    bread
1 cup gold raisins
1 cup dried apricots,
    ¼-inch dices
1 tsp. basil

1 tsp. sage
1 tsp. salt
¼ tsp. pepper
½ cup water
¼ cup butter
1 tsp. salt
¼ tsp. pepper

Preheat oven to 450°F.

Wash and dry Cornish hens. Set aside. Combine bread cubes, fruit and seasonings. Heat water and butter together until butter is melted. Pour over dry mixture. Toss lightly. Fill cavities of Cornish hens with stuffing. Season hens with salt and pepper. Cover exposed stuffing and ends of legs with aluminum foil during first half of roasting. Roast for 20 minutes; reduce heat to 350°F., and roast 60 to 75 minutes longer or until drumstick twists easily and birds are nicely browned. Baste several times.

Serves 6.

MOTHER DOWD'S

Skillet Luau

½ green pepper, cut into ¼-inch strips
1 clove garlic, minced
2 tsps. curry powder
2 Tbs. butter
1 can cream of chicken soup, undiluted, about 10¼ ozs.

½ cup water
2 cups cooked chicken, ½-inch cubes
½ cup pineapple tidbits, drained
Toasted slivered almonds for garnish

In heavy-bottomed saucepan, sauté pepper, garlic and curry in butter over low heat until peppers are tender. Add remaining ingredients. Bring to a boil stirring constantly.

Serve over rice. Garnish with toasted slivered almonds.

Serves 3 to 4.

MOTHER DOWD'S

Tamale Pie

1 cup yellow corn meal
4 cups hot water
1 tsp. salt
½ cup chopped onion
1 cup chopped green
    pepper
3 Tbs. olive oil

2½ cups tomatoes,
    or 20-oz. can
3 cups coarsely ground
    cooked chicken
1 tsp. salt
1 Tb. chili powder
Dash cayenne

Preheat oven to 375°F.

Cook corn meal, water and salt in top of double boiler 45 minutes, stirring occasionally.

Sauté onions and pepper in oil in frying pan or heavy-bottomed saucepan until lightly browned. Add remaining ingredients. Cook over low heat stirring constantly, until moisture evaporates (approximately 10 minutes).

Pour 2 cups corn meal mush into greased 9-inch square baking dish. Top first with chicken mixture and then remaining mush. Bake 30 to 45 minutes or until lightly browned.

Serves 6.

MOTHER DOWD'S

Yellow Rice and Chicken

1 frying chicken, approximately 2½ lbs.
1 tsp. salt
¼ tsp. pepper
½ cup oil
½ cup finely chopped onion
1 cup finely chopped green pepper
2 cloves garlic, crushed
1 cup rice
1 tsp. salt
1 bay leaf
¼ tsp. crushed saffron
3 cups hot water
1¼ cups tomatoes, crushed, or 14½-oz. can
¾ cup drained mushroom buttons (optional), or 4-oz. can
1 cup drained cooked peas, or 8-oz. can

Have butcher cut chicken into 2-inch pieces. Wash and dry chicken pieces. Season with salt and pepper. Over moderate heat fry in oil turning as necessary until golden brown (approximately 30 minutes) in 3-quart Dutch oven or frying pan. Add onions, green pepper and garlic and continue cooking until onions are transparent. Add remaining ingredients except peas. Stir. Bring to a boil. Cover and simmer 30 minutes or until rice is tender and moisture absorbed.

Garnish with peas.

Serves 6.

ANN CORIO'S

Chicken Cacciatore al Forno

2 frying chickens, about
   2½ lbs. each
1 Tb. salt
1 tsp. pepper
2 green peppers, cut
   into ¼-inch strips
½ lb. fresh mushrooms,
   sliced ¼-inch thick
2 cloves garlic, minced

2 bay leaves
½ cup olive oil
2½ cups Italian style to-
   matoes, crushed, or
   20-oz. can
2 Tbs. sugar
¼ cup Italian red wine
   (optional)

Preheat oven to 450°F.

Quarter chicken. Wash and dry. Season with salt and pepper. Place skin side down one layer deep in a shallow baking dish which has been coated with olive oil. Top with peppers, mushrooms, garlic and bay leaves. Sprinkle with olive oil. Bake 45 minutes, turning chicken once, or until it is browned. Combine tomatoes and sugar. Pour over chicken. Reduce heat to 400°F. Bake ½ hour. Add wine and bake 10 minutes longer or until chicken is tender.

Serves 8.

CAROL WALEK'S

Paella

Paella is best made in a paella pan, which resembles a large frying pan with gently sloping sides and two handles. It can be served in same pan. If not available, any large frying pan or Dutch oven will do. Only accompaniment necessary is plenty of salad.

3 lbs. chicken parts
½ cup olive oil
¼ lb. pepperoni
4 tomatoes, peeled and
    diced ½-inch thick
1 cup finely chopped
    onion
2 cloves garlic, minced
2 Tbs. chopped parsley
1 tsp. paprika
2 tsps. salt
10 threads saffron
¼ tsp. pepper

1½ cups raw rice
3 cups chicken broth
1 package frozen artichokes
    (optional), 9 ozs.
2 pimientos, sliced into
    ¼-inch strips
12 clams or mussels
½ lb. shrimp
½ lb. lobster pieces or
    squid
1 package frozen peas,
    10 ozs.

Wash and dry chicken. Cut into 2-inch pieces. In 14-inch paella pan, brown chicken on all sides over moderate heat in oil (approximately 20 minutes). Remove chicken and set aside. Add pepperoni, tomatoes, onions and garlic and cook 10 minutes longer, stirring frequently. Add seasonings and rice. Stir until rice is well coated with oil. Add broth. Arrange chicken and remaining ingredients except peas on top of rice. Cover and simmer 30 minutes. Add peas and continue to cook until rice is tender and moisture absorbed.

Serves 8.

WALTER JETTON'S
(LBJ'S BBQ CHEF)
Poultry Seasoning

3 Tbs. salt
1½ Tbs. black pepper
1 Tb. monosodium
   glutamate

½ Tb. garlic powder
½ tsp. ground bay leaves
3 Tbs. paprika
1 Tb. dry mustard

Combine spices together. Allow 1 teaspoon per pound of chicken. Rub on chicken. Broil, bake, fry or braise as desired.

*

Seafood

---

*

HOWARD DUFF'S

Crab Duff

4 scallions, chopped, or
½ cup chopped
onion
¼ cup butter
1¾ cups tomatoes,
crushed, or 1-lb. can

1 can crab meat, 6½ ozs.
6 eggs, separated
¼ cup milk
½ tsp. salt
¼ tsp. pepper

Sauté onions in butter in 12-inch heavy skillet until transparent. Add tomatoes. Cook ½ hour over low heat, stirring occasionally. Add crab meat.

Meanwhile, beat egg whites until stiff but not dry. Combine yolks, milk, salt and pepper and beat until light colored. Fold yolk mixture into whites. Pour egg mixture over crab mixture. Cook over *low* heat, stirring constantly, 3 to 4 minutes or until firm.

Serves 6.

PHYLLIS DILLER'S

Scalloped Oysters

2 cups freshly rolled
cracker crumbs
1 pt. whole oysters,
drained
¼ lb. butter

½ cup heavy cream
1 tsp. salt
⅛ tsp. pepper
⅛ tsp. nutmeg

Preheat oven to 425°F.

Cover bottom of greased 1½-quart baking dish with ⅔ cup cracker crumbs. Top with 1 cup oysters. Dot with ⅓ of butter. Repeat. Combine cream and seasonings. Pour over casserole. Top finally with cracker crumbs and dot with remaining butter. Bake 20 to 25 minutes.

Serves 6 to 8.

MOTHER DOWD'S

Big Catch Casserole

2 cups dry noodles
1 can cream of celery
   soup, undiluted,
   about 10¼ oz.
½ cup salad dressing
¼ cup milk
¼ cup grated
   Parmesan cheese

1 can salmon, 1 lb.,
   drained, flaked
1 package frozen peas,
   10 ozs., thawed
1 Tb. minced onion

Preheat oven to 350°F.

Cook noodles according to package instructions. Drain, rinse and set aside.

Combine soup, salad dressing, milk and cheese. Blend well. Add noodles and remaining ingredients. Pour into greased 1½-quart casserole. Bake 45 minutes or until bubbling.

May be topped with buttered crumbs or cheese.

Serves 4 to 6.

PETER LIND HAYES'S AND MARY HEALY'S

Shrimp À La Creole

3 lbs. peeled and
   deveined shrimp
1 Tb. salt
Cold water to cover
3 Tbs. flour
½ cup salad oil
6 shallots, chopped, or
   1 cup chopped
   onions

4 cups chopped green
   pepper
¾ cup tomato paste,
   6-oz. can
2 tsps. salt
½ tsp. black pepper

Place shrimp, salt and water in pot. Bring to a boil. Remove from heat. Allow shrimp to remain in hot water 5 minutes. Remove shrimp. Save stock.

Meanwhile cook flour and oil in large heavy-bottomed skillet until lightly browned, stirring occasionally. Add shallots or onions and peppers. Cook 15 minutes or until onions are lightly browned and peppers tender. Add tomato paste, 2 cups stock, salt and pepper. Cover and cook over low heat 45 minutes. Add shrimp and cook 10 minutes longer.

Serve over rice.

Serves 10 to 12.

GEORGE KIRBY'S

Shrimp A La George Kirby

1 lb. peeled and deveined shrimp	¼ tsp. pepper
	Cold water to cover
1 tsp. garlic salt	2 Tbs. butter
1 tsp. onion salt	2 Tbs. flour
1 tsp. celery salt	1 tsp. dry mustard

Place shrimp, seasoning and water in saucepan. Bring to a boil. Remove from heat. Allow shrimp to remain in hot water 5 minutes. Remove shrimp. Save stock.

Melt butter. Add flour, stirring constantly. Cook slowly over very low heat for 5 to 10 minutes. Add 1 cup fish stock and mustard. Continue cooking, stirring constantly until thickened.

Serve sauce as an accompaniment to shrimp. Rice is a good accompaniment.

Serves 4.

MOTHER DOWD'S

Tuna Timbales

1 Tb. butter	½ tsp. salt
1 Tb. flour	¼ tsp. pepper
1 cup milk	2 eggs, beaten
2 cans flaked tuna,	2 Tbs. lemon juice
6½ ozs. each	½ cup milk
1 cup bread crumbs	1 cup grated Cheddar
1 Tb. chopped parsley	cheese, 4 ozs.

Preheat oven to 325°F.

Melt butter over low heat. Add flour, stirring constantly. Cook 10 minutes. Add milk. Stir until thickened. Toss cream sauce and all other ingredients except cheese together lightly. Place 1 cup in each individual baking dish or shells. Top each with ¼ cup grated cheese. Bake for 30 to 45 minutes or until cheese is lightly browned.

Serves 6.

NOTE: If you have a saltwater fisherman in your house, tell him to go catch a tuna so that you can use 2 cups of fresh flakes instead of the canned fish.

ILKA CHASE'S

Fish Stew

4 fresh shallots,	1 tsp. salt
finely chopped	⅛ tsp. white pepper
2 Tbs. butter	1½ lbs. white fish (sole,
2 cups light cream	scrod, flounder,
1 can minced clams,	haddock)
8 ozs., drained	¼ cup bread crumbs

Preheat oven to 350°F.

Sauté shallots in butter until transparent. Do not brown. Combine with cream, drained clams, salt and pepper. Cut fish into 1-inch pieces. Place in 1½-quart casserole. Pour clam mixture over fish. Top with crumbs. Bake ½ hour or until fish is done.

Serves 4.

Water Broiling: *A Little-Known Delight*

When Dan Morris appeared on *The Mike Douglas Show* in connection with the publication of his seafood cookbook "The Savor of the Sea," which he wrote with Matilda Moore and which Macmillan published in 1966, he described a little-known method of fish cookery that roused a lot of interest among our viewers.

It's called water broiling, a simple procedure whereby the fish, after only five minutes in the broiler, comes out steamed on the bottom and crunchy crisp on top. The first time Dan served it his daughter, who until then didn't like fish, exclaimed: "Oh boy, it tastes like candy!" and asked for a second helping.

It makes no difference what fish you use. Fresh caught and whatever is in season is best, but frozen fish will do almost as well. Now the step-by-step directions:

1. Cut larger fish into steaks or fillets about ½ inch thick; split small fish in two.

2. Place them on a wire (or otherwise perforated) rack in a shallow broiling pan and sprinkle the top side only generously with dried bread crumbs and dot with butter or margarine. Do *not* use cracker crumbs or corn meal.

3. Add about ⅛ to ¼ inch of hot water to the pan, making sure it does not touch the fish. This is the only liquid needed to bring out the flavor but if you like you can substitute milk, cream, wine, beer, or a fish, beef or chicken broth. If you want to add herbs or seasonings, do so to the liquid and not to the fish.

4. Preheat broiler to 550°F.

5. Slide pan into the broiler, making sure the fish is about 4 inches below the source of the heat.

6. Broil for about 5 minutes, less if the fish is less than ½ inch thick, more if it's thicker. In any case, a fork is a better test for doneness than a clock. Probe the flesh gently with the tines; when it flakes the fish is ready to be served. Another test: the fish should be done when the crumbs turn a rich golden brown.

VARIATIONS: Bulky vegetables make an excellent substitute for the wire rack, at the same time providing you with a balanced one-step meal. Using spinach as an example, spread hot, freshly cooked (frozen or canned will do) to cover the bottom of the broiling pan well, add the water, lay your fish on the spinach and then proceed as above.

*

Vegetables

---

*

A WORD TO THE WIVES

If you want your son (or your husband) to be President some-day then you'd better make sure that he eats his vegetables.

The thought first struck us when Lady Bird Johnson was our nation's First Lady. We asked her for a family favorite and the recipe that she gave us had spinach as its main ingredient. Then, when Pat Nixon was our First Lady-elect, came the clincher. We asked her for a family favorite and the recipe that she gave us had corn as its main ingredient.

Both vegetables!

But the similarity did not stop there; not only were their recipes for vegetable dishes, but both of them were for soufflés!

So, if you want your son (or your husband) to be President, make sure that he eats his vegetables and, as for you, learn how to bake them into a soufflé. And then, if he does not become President, you obviously need more practice.

LADY BIRD JOHNSON'S

Spinach Soufflé

2 packages frozen
   chopped spinach,
   10 ozs. each
¼ cup butter
¼ cup flour
Milk as needed
   (approximately 1½
   cups)

1 cup grated Cheddar
   cheese, 4 ozs.
Dash nutmeg
1 tsp. salt
⅛ tsp. pepper
1 Tb. sugar
1 tsp. grated onion
5 eggs, separated

Preheat oven to 375°F.

Thaw spinach. Drain. Reserve liquid. Add enough milk to liquid to make 2 cups.

Melt butter over low heat. Add flour. Blend well. Cook 10 minutes, stirring occasionally. Add milk gradually, stirring constantly. Cook until thick. Add spinach and remaining ingredients except eggs. Cook 4 to 5 minutes over low heat, stirring occasionally to prevent scorching. Remove from heat. Beat egg yolks until thick. Add equal amount of spinach mixture. Blend well. Add to first spinach mixture.

Beat egg whites until stiff but not dry. Fold spinach mixture into egg whites. Pour into greased 2-quart casserole. Set in pan containing 1 inch of hot water and bake 40 to 50 minutes or until table knife inserted 2 inches from edge comes out clean.

Serves 6.

PAT NIXON'S
Corn Soufflé

2 Tbs. butter	1 cup half & half
2 Tbs. flour	3 eggs, separated
1½ tsps. salt	2 cups cream style corn,
¼ tsp. white pepper	16-oz. can

Preheat oven to 350°F.

Melt butter in heavy saucepan. Add flour. Mix until well combined. Cook over low heat, stirring occasionally, for 10 minutes. *Do not brown.* Add seasonings and half & half. Cook over moderate heat, stirring constantly, until thick. Remove from heat. Beat egg yolks until foamy. Add equal amount of cream sauce and mix well. Add to remaining cream sauce and mix until well blended. Add corn and mix until just combined.

Beat whites until stiff but not dry. Fold corn mixture into whites. Pour into greased 2-quart casserole. Bake 30 minutes or until table knife inserted 2 inches from edge comes out clean.

Serves 6.

ANNA MOFFO'S

All' Arrabbiate

¼ cup butter
½ lb. sliced bacon cut
   into 1-inch squares
½ lb. fresh mushrooms
   sliced ¼ inch thick
2 cloves garlic

½ dry hot pepper
3½ cups tomatoes, crushed,
   or 30-oz. can
¾ tsp. salt
½ tsp. sweet basil
½ lb. rigatoni

Sauté bacon and mushrooms in butter until bacon is crisp. Remove bacon and mushrooms and set aside. Brown garlic and red pepper. Remove and discard. Add tomatoes to fat; cook 30 minutes over low heat. Add bacon, mushrooms, salt and basil. Cook 15 minutes longer.

Prepare rigatoni according to package instructions. Serve sauce over rigatoni.

Serves 4.

MARILYN MITCHELL'S (MRS. AMERICA)

Almond Rice Parisian

½ cup rice
½ cup sliced almonds
½ cup sliced mush-
   rooms, drained,
   or 4-oz. can

3 Tbs. butter
1 can onion soup, undi-
   luted, about 10¼ ozs.
⅔ cup hot water

Over moderate heat brown rice, almonds and mushrooms in butter in heavy-bottomed pot or skillet (approximately 10 minutes), stirring frequently. Add soup and water; stir. Bring to a boil. Reduce heat, cover and cook 25 minutes or until liquid is absorbed and rice is tender.

Serves 6.

ARTHUR GODFREY'S

Beans Deluxe

4 cups baked beans, or 2 cans, 1 lb. each	4 slices bacon ½ cup dark brown sugar

Preheat oven to 350°F.

Empty beans into 1-quart casserole or square baking dish. Top with bacon (avoid bacon overlapping) and then sugar. Cover and bake for 30 minutes. Uncover and continue baking 30 minutes or until bacon is done.

Serves 6.

PHYLLIS DILLER'S

Fried Cucumbers

2 cucumbers ⅓ cup flour	Bacon fat Salt and pepper to taste

Pare cucumbers. Cut in half crosswise and slice lengthwise into ½-inch-thick slices. Dredge in flour. Fry in bacon fat in skillet until golden brown and tender. Season to taste.

Serves 6.

RECIPES

CONNIE FRANCIS'S
Eggplant Parmesan

2 cloves garlic, minced
2 Tbs. olive oil
3½ cups Italian tomatoes, or 30-oz. can
3½ cups tomato sauce, or 30-oz. can
1 tsp. oregano
1 tsp. basil
1 tsp. salt
¼ tsp. pepper
½ cup grated Parmesan cheese

2 eggs, well beaten
1 Tb. grated Parmesan cheese
1 eggplant, peeled, sliced crosswise ¼ inch thick
1 cup Italian seasoned bread crumbs
¾ cup olive oil
¼ lb. sliced mozzarella cheese

Preheat oven to 325°F.

Sauté garlic in oil in 2-quart saucepan until lightly browned. Add tomatoes, tomato sauce and seasonings. Cover and simmer slowly 45 minutes. Add Parmesan cheese. Set aside.

Combine beaten eggs and Parmesan cheese. Dip eggplant first in eggs and then crumbs. Sauté in hot olive oil until golden brown on both sides. Place layer of eggplant in greased 2-quart casserole; top with mozzarella and tomato sauce. Repeat until all eggplant is used, topping last layer with cheese. Bake, uncovered, 30 to 40 minutes until sauce is bubbly and cheese melted.

Serves 4 to 6.

FRANKIE LAINE'S

Stuffed Eggplant

1 eggplant, 2 to 2½ lbs.
1 lb. mushrooms
¼ cup chopped green
    pepper
6 green onions,
    chopped
2 cloves garlic, crushed
½ lb. ground sirloin
¼ cup cooking oil

1 cup red wine
½ tsp. oregano
1 Tb. parsley
½ tsp. paprika
2 tsps. salt
¼ tsp. pepper
¼ cup Parmesan cheese
4 slices mozzarella cheese

Preheat oven to 350°F.

Wash eggplant. Cut in half lengthwise. Scoop out pulp leaving ½-inch shell. Dice pulp.

Sauté eggplant pulp, mushrooms, green pepper, onion, garlic and meat in oil in a large skillet until meat is browned. Add remaining ingredients except mozzarella cheese. Cook about ½ hour or until most of moisture is absorbed. Fill eggplant shells. Top with mozzarella cheese. Place in baking pan to which ¼ cup of water has been added. Bake 30 to 40 minutes or until eggplant is tender and cheese is melted.

Serves 4.

NOTE: When a fine singer like Frankie Laine performs it's rare for viewers to see his piano accompanist. But when Frankie demonstrated this recipe, Ray Barr, his pianist, was very much present for all to see. Showing that singers look to their accompanists for more than just musical accompaniment. Especially when it comes to cooking.

GENEVIEVE'S

Sautéed Mushrooms

2 Tbs. butter	½ lb. fresh mushrooms,
1 Tb. oil	whole, sliced or
	quartered

Heat butter and oil over high heat until butter stops foaming. Add mushrooms and sauté, stirring constantly, 4 to 5 minutes or until lightly browned.

Serves 4 as an accompaniment to meat or vegetable garnish.

ANITA BRYANT'S AND BOB GREEN'S

Florida Orange-Carrot Ring

3 lbs. carrots	3 eggs, well beaten
Water to cover	1½ Tbs. flour
2 tsps. salt	½ cup orange juice
½ Tb. finely minced	1 Tb. grated orange rind
onion	1 cup light cream
3 Tbs. melted butter	1 tsp. salt

Preheat oven to 350°F.

Pare carrots and slice into ½-inch rings. Add to boiling salted water. Cover and simmer 30 to 40 minutes or until very tender. Drain. Purée in food mill or force through sieve (yield: 3½ cups). Combine carrots with remaining ingredients. Pour into well-greased 6-cup ring mold.

Place mold in pan with ½ inch of hot water. Bake 1 hour or until table knife inserted 1 inch from edge comes out clean. Carefully run knife around edge of ring. Let stand 5 minutes before unmolding. Invert on serving platter; remove mold. Fill center with peas and mushrooms or another vegetable of complementary color.

Serves 12.

STAN HURWITZ'S

String Bean Casserole

3 packages frozen
French-style green
beans, 9 ozs. each
3 cans cream of mush-
room soup,
10¼ ozs. each

6 cups (3 cans) fried onion
rings, 3½ ozs. each

Preheat oven to 300°F.

Cook green beans in boiling salted water for 5 minutes; drain. Place ⅓ of beans in 1½-quart casserole. Pour 1 can *undiluted* soup over it and top with onion rings. Repeat 3 times to form layers.

Bake 30 to 35 minutes or until onion rings are crisp, and mixture is hot and bubbly.

Serves 16.

GENEVIEVE'S

Sweet Potatoes in Orange Cups

4 California oranges
1¼ lbs. sweet potatoes
1 egg, beaten
½ cup light cream

2 Tbs. butter
½ tsp. salt
1/16 tsp. nutmeg
4 marshmallows (optional)

Preheat oven to 350°F.

To scoop out oranges, cut stem end off crosswise. Using paring knife, remove entire pulp from fruit. Refrigerate until needed.

Scrub and peel potatoes. Cook in boiling salted water to cover 20 to 25 minutes or until tender. Mash. Add orange pulp and remaining ingredients except marshmallows. Whip until light. Fill orange cups. Garnish with marshmallow if desired. Bake 20 minutes.

Serves 4.

NOTE: Filling may also be baked in 1-quart greased casserole.

PHYLLIS DILLER'S
Tomato Ding Ding Recipe

2½ cups tomatoes,
    crushed, or 20-oz.
    can
2 slices stale white
    bread, diced into
    ½-inch pieces

½ cup brown sugar
¼ cup butter
½ tsp. salt
⅛ tsp. pepper

Combine all ingredients in saucepan or 1-quart baking dish. Cook over low heat or in 350°F. oven 15 minutes or until hot.
Serves 6.

GENEVIEVE'S
Zucchini Casserole

2 lbs. zucchini sliced
    crosswise, ½-inch
    thick slices
1 cup water
½ tsp. salt

¼ cup light cream
1 egg, beaten
¼ cup melted butter
½ cup grated Parmesan
    cheese

Preheat oven to 375°F.
Add zucchini to boiling salted water. Cover and simmer 10 minutes or until tender. Drain.
Place zucchini in 1½-quart greased casserole. Combine cream, beaten egg, melted butter and ¼ cup of cheese. Pour over zucchini. Sprinkle remaining cheese on top. Bake 25 minutes or until cheese is golden brown.
Serves 8.

*

Breads,
Cakes,
Cookies,
and Cornpone

*

Eggs and flour are called for in most, if not all, of the recipes that follow. Unless otherwise specified, the eggs are always large and the flour is all-purpose.

GENEVIEVE'S

Applesauce Nut Bread

2 cups sifted flour	1 cup chopped walnuts
¾ cup sugar	1 egg, beaten
1 Tb. baking powder	1 cup applesauce
½ tsp. cinnamon	2 Tbs. melted shortening
½ tsp. baking soda	or oil
1 tsp. salt	

Preheat oven to 350°F.

Sift together dry ingredients into mixing bowl. Add nuts and mix. Make well in mixture. Add remaining ingredients. Mix until blended. Pour into greased and floured 5 x 9 x 3-inch loaf pan.

Bake 1 hour or until done. Remove from pan 10 minutes after it comes from oven to prevent sogginess.

Makes 1 loaf.

GENEVIEVE'S
Banana Bread

2 cups flour
1 tsp. baking soda
¼ tsp. salt
½ cup butter
1 cup sugar

2 eggs
1 cup mashed bananas
   (2 to 3 ripe bananas)
¾ cup chopped nut meats

Preheat oven to 350°F.

Sift flour, baking soda, and salt together; set aside. Cream butter until light. Add sugar gradually. Beat until creamy. Add eggs and beat until lemon colored and fluffy. Add flour mixture alternately with bananas. Add nuts; mix to combine. Pour into greased 9 x 5 x 3-inch loaf pan.

Bake 1 hour or until done.

Makes 1 loaf.

BOB CROSBY'S
Carrot Bread

2 cups sifted flour
1½ cups sugar
2 tsps. cinnamon
2 tsps. baking powder
1 tsp. salt
¼ cup chopped walnuts

2 cups finely grated carrots
½ cup shredded coconut
½ cup seedless raisins
1 cup oil
1 tsp. vanilla
3 eggs, beaten

Preheat oven to 350°F.

Sift dry ingredients together into mixing bowl. Make well in center. Add remaining ingredients. Stir until well combined. Pour into greased 9 x 5 x 3-inch loaf pan. Set aside 20 minutes to prevent crumbling after baking. Bake for 1 hour or until done. Remove from pan to cool.

Makes 1 loaf.

CAROL WALEK'S
Cinnamon Buns

2 cups milk
¼ lb. butter
¾ cup sugar
1 tsp. salt
2 eggs, well beaten
1 pkg. dry yeast

¼ cup hot tap water
8 cups flour
2 cups sugar
⅓ cup Saigon cinnamon
½ lb. butter, melted

Preheat oven to 350°F.

Scald milk; add butter, sugar and salt. Cool to lukewarm. Add beaten eggs and yeast which has been dissolved in water according to instructions on package. Stir in 6 cups flour and beat until smooth. Turn out batter onto floured board and gently knead in the remaining 2 cups flour. Place dough in bowl. Cover with a towel. Set aside in a warm place until dough is double in bulk.

Turn out onto lightly floured board and knead for ½ minute. Divide dough in 2 parts. Roll 1 part into an oblong 8 x 18 x ¼ inch thick. Combine sugar and cinnamon. Spread ½ cup melted butter on dough. Sprinkle with 1 cup cinnamon mixture. Roll like jelly roll. Cut crosswise into 1-inch slices, place on lightly greased sheet pan allowing 1 inch between. Repeat for other ½ of dough. Let rise until light. Brush with beaten egg. Bake for 25 minutes or until hollow sounding when tapped.

Makes 3 dozen buns.

FROSTING

2 cup confectioners'
    sugar
Dash salt

1 tsp. vanilla
Enough milk to spread

Combine sugar, salt and vanilla. Add enough milk to make it spreading consistency. Spread over cooled buns.

BOBBY GENTRY'S
Grandma's Corn Bread

1 cup yellow corn meal	2 eggs, lightly beaten
1 cup sifted flour	¾ cup buttermilk
2 tsps. baking powder	¼ cup melted shortening
1 tsp. salt	

Preheat oven to 400°F.

Sift together dry ingredients into mixing bowl. Add remaining ingredients and beat until smooth. Pour into greased 9-inch square baking pan or preheated greased 10-inch oven-proof skillet. Bake 20 to 25 minutes or until golden brown.

Serves 9.

GRANDPA JONES'S
Corn Bread *

2 cups white corn meal	1 egg, beaten
1 tsp. baking powder	¼ cup bacon drippings,
1 Tb. sugar	melted
¼ tsp. salt	1¼ cups milk
⅓ cup boiling water	

Preheat oven to 400°F.

Grease and heat muffin tins or corn-stick pan. Sift together dry ingredients into mixing bowl. Remove 2 Tbs. dry mixture to small bowl. Add boiling water and mix. Add remaining ingredients to dry ingredients. Mix until well blended. Add scalded ingredients. Fill hot muffin tins ⅔ full. Bake 18 to 20 minutes or until golden brown.

Makes 12 medium-sized muffins or 14 corn sticks.

NOTE: May also be baked in 9-inch square pan or 10-inch skillet.

* Some people, including even Grandpa Jones, might call this a recipe for corn pone. But we're big-time sophisticates up here in Philadelphia.

MINNIE PEARL'S
Corn Light Bread

3 cups white corn meal
¾ cup flour
1 cup sugar
1 tsp. salt

½ tsp. baking soda
1 tsp. baking powder
3 cups buttermilk
½ cup oil

Preheat oven to 400°F.

Mix dry ingredients together in bowl. Make well in center, add remaining ingredients. Mix until well combined. Pour into greased tube pan. Bake 1 hour or until done.

Makes 1 loaf.

CAROL CHANNING'S
Hello Dolly Cookies

½ cup butter
1 cup graham cracker
    crumbs
1 cup coconut
1 cup chopped nutmeats

1 package chocolate chips,
    6 ozs.
1 can sweetened condensed
    milk

Preheat oven to 350°F.

Melt butter in 9 x 12-inch baking pan.

Spread remaining ingredients in pan in order given. Bake 25 minutes or until lightly browned on top. Cool completely. Cut into 1½-inch squares.

Makes 48 squares.

NOTE: These cookies will go well at Harriet Van Horne's Dinner Party (see page 88). Miss Channing, meet Miss Van Horne.

MOTHER DOWD'S

Corn Flakes or Wheaties Cookies

2 cups sifted flour
½ tsp. salt
2 tsps. baking powder
1 cup soft shortening
1 cup sugar
1 cup packed brown
   sugar

2 eggs
1 tsp. vanilla
2 cups Corn Flakes or
   Wheaties
1 cup coconut or chopped
   nutmeats

Preheat oven to 375°F.

Sift flour, salt, and baking powder together. Cream shortening and sugar. Add eggs, one at a time, and then vanilla, beating until light after each addition. Add sifted dry ingredients, cereal and nuts; mix well. Drop by teaspoonfuls onto greased cookie sheets; bake 10 to 12 minutes.

Makes 6 dozen.

GENEVIEVE'S

Orange Cookies

4 cups sifted flour
1½ tsps. baking powder
1 tsp. baking soda
¾ tsp. salt
¾ cup soft butter
1½ cups packed brown
   sugar

2 eggs
1 tsp. vanilla
½ cup sour milk
¾ cup chopped nutmeats
3 Tbs. grated orange rind

Preheat oven to 375°F.

Sift flour, baking powder, soda, and salt together. Cream butter and sugar. Add eggs, one at a time, and then vanilla, beating until light after each addition. Add sifted dry ingredients, milk, nuts and grated rind; mix well. Drop by teaspoonfuls onto greased cookie sheets; bake 10 to 12 minutes.

While hot, glaze with sauce made by combining the following:

1 cup sugar 2 Tbs. grated orange rind
⅓ cup orange juice

Makes 6 dozen.

MOTHER DOWD'S
Swedish Christmas Cookies

6 eggs ¾ cup sugar
2 cups sifted flour ½ tsp. lemon extract
½ tsp. salt 3 Tbs. light cream
¾ cup shortening

Preheat oven to 375°F.

Separate yolks from whites. Do not break yolks. Drop yolks from saucer into simmering salted water. Simmer 7 to 10 minutes or until hard cooked. Remove from water with slotted spoon. Cool and then sieve.

Sift flour and salt together. Cream shortening and sugar until light and fluffy. Add sieved egg yolk and extract; mix. Add dry ingredients alternately with cream beating well after each addition.

On lightly floured board, roll dough ⅛ inch thick. Cut with Christmas-shaped cookie cutters. Place 2 inches apart on greased cookie sheet. Decorate with red and green sugar.

Bake 8 to 10 minutes or until edges become lightly browned.

Makes 3 dozen.

GENEVIEVE'S

Sandies

1 cup soft butter	¼ tsp. salt
¼ cup powdered sugar	2½ cups sifted flour
2 tsps. vanilla	1 cup chopped pecans
1 Tb. water	Powdered sugar

Preheat oven to 300°F.

Combine ingredients in order listed beating well after each addition. Form into 1-inch balls. Bake 2 inches apart on ungreased cookie sheet 25 to 30 minutes or until lightly browned. Roll in powdered sugar while warm.

Makes 5 dozen.

CAROL LAWRENCE'S

"Tree" Cookie

¾ cup plus 2 Tbs. eggs	1 Tb. ground aniseed
2¼ cups sugar	4 cups sifted flour
1 Tb. kirsch	

Beat eggs, sugar, kirsch and aniseed until light and lemon colored. Add flour; mix until combined. Knead on lightly floured board until smooth. Roll ½ inch thick. Cut into desired shapes with cookie cutter. Place on greased cookie sheet. Insert toothpick in each cookie to make small hole by which cookie can be threaded and hung on tree. Allow cookies to dry for 2 days before baking.

Preheat oven to 325°F. Remove toothpicks. Bake 25 minutes. Cool cookies. Brush with food coloring to decorate.

MOTHER DOWD'S

Butter Pecan Crescents

2 cups sifted flour	6 Tbs. powdered sugar
½ tsp. salt	2 tsps. vanilla
1 cup soft butter	1 cup chopped pecans

Preheat oven to 350°F.

Sift flour and salt together. Cream butter and sugar until light and fluffy. Add vanilla. Blend well. Add flour; mix until well blended. Add nuts. Shape dough into 2-inch rolls the thickness of a pencil. Shape into crescents 2 inches apart on lightly greased cookie sheet. Bake 15 to 20 minutes or until lightly browned. Dust with powdered sugar while still warm.

Makes 4 dozen.

MOTHER DOWD'S

Cream Cheese Kolacky

1 cup soft butter	2 tsps. baking powder
9 ozs. soft cream cheese	¼ tsp. salt
2 eggs, well beaten	2 cups prune, apricot,
2 Tbs. sugar	cheese or poppy seed
2 cups sifted flour	filling

Cream butter, cream cheese and eggs; add sugar and mix until light. Stir dry ingredients into cheese mixture. Shape into a ball. Wrap in waxed paper or foil and chill overnight in refrigerator.

Preheat oven to 375°F.

Roll dough out ⅛ inch thick on floured board. Cut into 1½-inch squares or 2-inch rounds. Place on ungreased cookie sheet. Fill with 1 tsp. of filling of your choice or sprinkle with cinnamon sugar. Bake 15 to 18 minutes or until delicately brown.

Makes 6 dozen.

GYPSY ROSE LEE'S

Torrijas

1 loaf French bread	1 tsp. vanilla
(14 to 16 inch)	4 eggs, beaten
1 qt. milk	2 Tbs. sugar
2 eggs, beaten	Olive oil
⅛ tsp. nutmeg	Powdered sugar
¼ cup sugar	

Cut bread into 1-inch-thick slices. Dry overnight or longer.

Combine milk, 2 eggs, nutmeg, sugar and vanilla. Place dried bread one layer deep in shallow baking dish. Pour egg mixture over bread and allow to soak 3 to 4 hours or until egg mixture is almost absorbed.

Beat together 4 eggs and sugar. Remove bread carefully and dip in beaten egg mixture. Fry in ½ inch olive oil over moderate heat until golden brown. Turn. Drain. Sprinkle with powdered sugar.

GENEVIEVE'S

Four Waffles

1½ cups flour	2 eggs, separated
1 Tb. baking powder	1¼ cups milk
1 tsp. salt	⅓ cup melted butter

Preheat waffle iron to hot.

Sift dry ingredients together. Set aside.

Beat egg whites stiff *but not dry*. Set aside. In large mixing bowl, beat yolks. Add milk and then dry ingredients. Mix until just combined. Add melted butter and mix. Fold in egg whites.

Pour 1 cup into hot waffle iron. Bake until golden brown.

Makes 4 waffles.

ROSE MARIE'S

Dream Cake

½ cup soft shortening
½ cup soft butter
½ cup brown sugar
2 cups flour
¼ tsp. salt

4 eggs
1 cup sugar
1 tsp. vanilla
2 cups chopped walnuts
2⅔ cups coconut, 7 ozs.

Preheat oven to 350°F.

Combine shortening, butter, brown sugar, flour and salt. Press firmly into ungreased 9 x 13 x 2-inch oblong cake pan. Bake 15 minutes.

Meanwhile, beat eggs until light. Add sugar gradually, beating constantly until thick and lemon colored. Add vanilla. Fold in nuts and coconut. Spread over baked mixture in pan. Bake 20 to 25 minutes or until golden brown. Cut into 2-inch squares.

Makes 24 squares.

MOTHER DOWD'S

Butter Cake

½ cup finely chopped
  nutmeats
1 cup soft butter
1 cup plus 2 Tbs. sugar

1 cup eggs, slightly beaten
1 tsp. vanilla
2½ cups sifted cake flour
¼ tsp. salt

Preheat oven to 275°F.

Spread nutmeats on sides and bottom of well-buttered 10-inch spring form cheesecake pan. Cream butter and sugar together until light and fluffy. Add eggs and vanilla gradually and beat until thick and lemon colored (about 15 minutes total).

Sift flour and salt 4 to 5 times. Add flour a little at a time to egg mixture, beating just enough to blend in flour after each addition. Pour batter into pan. Bake 2½ hours or until done.

Cool before removing from pan.

Makes 1 cake.

MOTHER DOWD'S

Carrot Cake

3 cups sifted flour	1½ cups sugar
1 tsp. baking soda	4 eggs
1 tsp. baking powder	½ cup chopped nutmeats
1 tsp. salt	2 cups finely grated or
2 tsps. cinnamon	ground carrots
1½ cups oil	

Preheat oven to 350°F.

Sift together dry ingredients. Set aside.

Beat oil and sugar together. Add eggs one at a time, beating well after each addition. Continue beating until light and lemon colored. Add dry ingredients, nuts and carrots and mix until well combined.

Pour into greased 10-inch tube pan. Bake 1 hour or until done. Remove from pan to cool.

Makes 1 cake.

GENEVIEVE'S AUNT MARGENE'S

Buttermilk Chocolate Cake

2½ cups sifted flour	1 tsp. vanilla
1 tsp. baking soda	5 eggs, separated
½ tsp. salt	4 squares unsweetened
1 cup soft butter	chocolate, melted
2 cups sugar	1 cup buttermilk

Preheat oven to 350°F.

Sift flour, soda, and salt together. Set aside.

Cream butter and sugar together until light and fluffy. Add vanilla and egg yolks, one at a time, beating after each addition until fluffy. Continue beating until thick and lemon colored. Add melted chocolate and mix until well blended. Add sifted dry ingredients alternately with buttermilk, beginning and ending with dry ingredients. Mix after each addition. Beat egg whites until stiff but not dry. Fold chocolate mixture into whites. Pour into greased and floured 9 x 13 x 2-inch baking pan.

Bake 35 minutes or until done.

Serves 20.

ICING

1/4 cup butter
3 squares unsweetened
     chocolate
1 lb. powdered sugar,
     sifted

1/3 cup half & half
1 tsp. vanilla
1 egg yolk, well beaten

Melt butter and chocolate together. Combine all ingredients and beat until creamy. Spread on cake while still warm.

MADELEINE KAMMAN'S
Mexican Cake

CAKE

1/2 cup sifted flour
3/4 cup sifted cocoa
5 eggs
2/3 cup sugar

10 Tbs. melted unsalted
     butter, or 1/2 cup plus
     2 Tbs.

Preheat oven to 325°F.

Sift flour and cocoa together once. Beat eggs and sugar together until light lemon colored and creamy. Fold flour-cocoa mixture directly from sifter into egg mixture. Last fold in melted butter. Pour batter into well-greased and lightly floured 8-inch baking pan. Bake 40 to 45 minutes or until done. Remove from pan immediately. Cool on rack before filling.

FILLING

2 egg yolks	2 Tbs. cocoa
⅓ cup sifted powdered sugar	1 Tb. rum
	¼ cup soft butter

Beat egg yolks, sugar, cocoa and rum together until light and creamy. Add butter and beat until heavy spreading consistency. Cut cake into 2 layers and fill.

ICING

2 cups sifted powdered sugar	1 Tb. rum
2 Tbs. cocoa	2 Tbs. water (approximately)

Combine all ingredients. Add water gradually until thin spreading consistency. Frost top and sides of cake.

To decorate, mix ½ cup sifted powdered sugar and 2½ teaspoons water. Pipe circular decoration on cake. Draw lines from center to edges to make a spidery design.

Makes 1 cake.

VIRGINIA GRAHAM'S

Cheesecake

6-oz. package zwieback (2 cups crumbs)	1 cup sugar
½ cup sugar	1 cup sour cream
½ cup melted butter	2 tsps. lemon rind
1 lb. soft cream cheese	1 Tb. lemon juice
½ cup cottage cheese	1 tsp. vanilla
	5 eggs, separated

Preheat oven to 350°F.

Roll zwieback to make fine crumbs. Add sugar and butter and mix well with a fork. Set aside ½ cup. Press remaining crumb mixture on sides and bottom of 9-inch spring form pan. Combine remaining ingredients except eggs. Beat until smooth and creamy. Add egg yolks one at a time beating after each addition.

Beat whites until stiff but not dry. Fold cheese mixture into whites. Pour over crumb mixture.

Sprinkle ½ cup crumbs on top. Bake one hour. Turn off oven and allow cake to cool in oven (door closed) for one hour. Run spatula around edge of pan before releasing sides.

Serves 12.

GENEVIEVE'S

Cheesecake

1 cup fine graham cracker crumbs (10 double crackers)	½ cup sugar
	2 tsps. vanilla
¼ cup melted butter	1 cup cultured sour cream
12 ozs. soft cream cheese	¼ cup sugar
	½ tsp. vanilla
3 eggs, separated	Additional graham cracker crumbs for garnish

Preheat oven to 350°F.

Mix cracker crumbs and melted butter together. Spread on bottom of 8-inch cheesecake pan. Press down firmly. Set aside.

Beat cheese until light. Add yolks, one at a time, and mix until light after each addition. Add sugar and vanilla and continue beating until smooth. Set aside. Beat egg whites until stiff but not dry. Fold cheese mixture into whites. Pour into crumb-lined pan. Bake 45 minutes or until table knife inserted 1 inch from edge comes out clean. Remove from oven and cool 10 to 15 minutes on rack.

Meanwhile combine sour cream, sugar and vanilla. Spread over top of cheesecake. Garnish with graham cracker crumbs. Return to oven and bake 5 minutes longer. When cool, refrigerate until ready to serve.

Serves 8 to 10.

GINNY GRAHAM'S
1-2-3-4 Cake

1 cup soft butter	3 tsps. baking powder
2 cups sugar	2 dashes mace
3 cups unsifted flour	1 cup milk
4 eggs	

Preheat oven to 325°F.

Cream butter and sugar together until light and fluffy. Add eggs, one at a time, beating until fluffy after each addition. Continue beating until thick and lemon colored.

Sift remaining dry ingredients together. Add to creamed mixture alternately with milk beginning and ending with dry ingredients. Pour into greased 10-inch tube pan and bake 60 to 65 minutes or until done.

Cool and then frost with your favorite chocolate fudge icing.

Serves 10.

NANCY WILSON'S

Sour Cream Fudge Cake

½ cup butter	¼ cup water
2 squares unsweetened chocolate	2 eggs, well beaten
	2 cups sifted cake flour
1 cup cultured sour cream	1½ cups sugar
	1 tsp. baking soda
1 tsp. vanilla	1 tsp. salt

Preheat oven to 350°F.

Melt butter and chocolate together. Combine with remaining liquid ingredients in order listed. Sift dry ingredients together. Combine liquid and dry ingredients. Pour into greased 10-inch tube pan. Bake 50 to 55 minutes or until done.

Serves 10.

JOHN FORSYTHE'S

Prune and Apricot Cake

¾ cup chopped dried prunes	1 Tb. flour
¾ cup chopped dried apricots	1 Tb. cinnamon
	¾ cup soft shortening
Boiling water to cover	¾ cup sugar
2 cups sifted flour	2 eggs
2 tsps. baking powder	¾ cup milk
½ tsp. salt	1 tsp. vanilla
⅔ cup firmly packed brown sugar	6 Tbs. melted butter
	⅓ cup chopped walnuts

Preheat oven to 350°F.

Combine prunes and apricots in small bowl. Pour boiling water to cover over fruit mixture. Set aside for 5 minutes. Drain well. Set aside until needed.

Sift flour, baking powder and salt together. Set aside. Combine brown sugar, 1 Tb. flour and cinnamon together. Set aside.

In large mixing bowl, cream shortening and sugar together until light and fluffy. Add eggs, one at a time, beating until fluffy after each addition. Continue beating until thick and lemon colored. Add flour mixture alternately with milk and vanilla beginning and ending with flour. Beat until just combined. Fold in drained fruit.

Pour ⅓ batter into greased and floured 10-inch tube pan. Spread evenly. Sprinkle with ⅓ cinnamon mixture and 2 Tbs. butter. Repeat twice. Top with nuts. Bake 55 minutes or until done. Cool in pan on rack 25 minutes.

Remove from pan.

Serve warm.

Serves 12.

Desserts

ENZO STUARTI'S

Cream Di Mascherpone

1 lb. ricotta or creamed cottage cheese	2 Tbs. heavy cream
½ cup sugar	2 Tbs. Cognac
4 egg yolks	1 pt. raspberries or strawberries

In blender on high speed, beat cheese until smooth. Lower speed to medium and add remaining ingredients except berries slowly. Beat until very smooth and thick. Pour into 1-quart serving dish. Chill 4 hours or longer. Hull and wash berries. Drain well. Top cheese mixture with berries.

Serves 6.

ILKA CHASE'S

Fruit Dish

1 can dark sweet pitted cherries, 1 lb.	1 tsp. lemon rind
1 can freestone peach halves, 30 ozs.	Juice of 1 orange
1 can apricot halves, 30 ozs.	Juice of 1 lemon
1 Tb. orange rind	¼ cup rum
	1 cup slivered almonds
	2 Tbs. butter

Preheat oven to 325°F.

Drain cherries well. Place peach and apricot halves pit side up in shallow baking dish with juice (fruit should crowd the bottom of the dish.)

Add drained cherries, orange and lemon juice and grated rind. Bake 2½ hours. Add rum and continue baking ½ hour longer.

The fruit will be darkened and syrup the consistency of a conserve. Sauté almonds in butter until browned. Drain and discard butter. Add nuts to fruit. Store at room temperature.

Serves 6.

NOTE: May also be served as a meat accompaniment.

MOTHER DOWD'S
Holiday Dessert

1 pt. whipping cream
¼ tsp. salt
¾ tsp. vanilla
2 tsps. sugar
1 can fruit cocktail, *drained*, 30 ozs.
1 can crushed pineapple, *drained*, 8 ozs.

1 cup ½-inch diced marshmallows (or petite marshmallows)
½ cup chopped nutmeats (optional)
Maraschino cherries

Beat cream until thick. Add salt, vanilla and sugar and continue beating until beater leaves ridge in cream. Fold fruit, marshmallows, and nuts into cream. Serve in sherbet glasses. Garnish with maraschino cherries.

Serves 8.

TOTIE FIELDS'S
Fruit Mélange

3 cups cut-up fresh and/or canned fruit (except bananas)
½ cup white raisins

½ cup orange juice
½ cup chopped walnuts
½ cup coconut

Combine fruit and raisins. Chill overnight. Drain well. Add orange juice. Pour into serving dish, top with walnuts and coconut. Serves 6.

TOTIE FIELDS'S

Fruit Mellow

1 can fruit cocktail,
  30 ozs., *drained*

3 cups petite marshmallows
1 pt. cultured sour cream

Combine all ingredients. Chill at least 2 hours before serving. Serves 8.

DELLA REESE'S

Apple Pie

1 pkg. piecrust mix,
  about 10 ozs.
4 ozs. sliced American
  cheese
4 medium-sized red
  apples, about 2 lbs.
4 medium-sized green
  apples, about 2 lbs.

¼ cup butter
1 Tb. apple pie spice (or
  your own mixture)
1½ cups sugar
¼ cup honey
¼ cup heavy cream

Preheat oven to 400°F.

Make 2 piecrusts according to package directions. Line 10-inch piepan with 1 crust. Cover crust with cheese slices. Peel, core and cut apples into ¼- to ½-inch slices. Layer apple slices, butter, spice and sugar on top of cheese. Pour honey overall. Top with second crust. Cut several slits in crust. Pour cream over crust. Bake for 55 minutes or until crust is golden brown.

Serves 6.

DELLA REESE'S

Ice Cream Pie

PIECRUST

1¼ cups graham
   cracker crumbs

3 Tbs. sugar
⅓ cup melted butter

Preheat oven to 375°F.
Mix together all ingredients. Press firmly into a 10-inch piepan.
Bake 8 minutes. Cool before filling.

FILLING

2 qts. vanilla ice cream
⅓ cup Cognac

2 pts. fresh strawberries or
   2 cups sliced peaches
   (well drained)
Whipped cream

Blend ice cream and Cognac until smooth. Wash and hull
berries; cut them in half. Spread ½ of fruit on baked crust. Top
with ½ of ice cream. Repeat. Freeze until solid. Top with whipped
cream and serve frozen.
Serves 6 to 8.

LADY BIRD JOHNSON'S

Pecan Pie

½ pkg. pie crust mix
1¼ cups pecan halves
⅓ cup butter
¾ cup brown sugar
   firmly packed

½ tsp. salt
4 eggs
1¾ cups light corn syrup
1 tsp. vanilla

Preheat oven to 350°F.
Prepare crust according to package directions. Line 10-inch
piepan with crust. Spread nuts on crust. Cream butter, sugar and

salt together until fluffy. Add eggs and mix only until blended. Add syrup and vanilla. Pour syrup mixture over nuts. Bake 45 minutes or until completely puffed across top. Cool well before cutting.

Serves 6.

CAROL WALEK'S
Chocolate Soufflé

2½ squares unsweetened chocolate	1 cup milk
¼ cup sugar	½ tsp. salt
5 Tbs. hot water	5 eggs, separated
⅓ cup butter	¼ cup sugar
3 Tbs. flour	1 tsp. vanilla

Preheat oven to 325°F.

Melt chocolate over hot water. Add sugar and hot water. Blend well and set aside away from heat. Meanwhile melt butter over low heat. Add flour and blend well. Cook over low heat for 10 minutes stirring occasionally. Add milk and beat vigorously. Bring to a boil, stirring constantly. Combine this cream sauce, chocolate mixture and salt. Beat yolks until foamy. Combine with an equal amount of chocolate mixture; mix well. Add this to remaining chocolate mixture, blending well. Cool to lukewarm.

Beat egg whites until stiff but not dry. Add sugar and beat until glossy. Add vanilla. Combine ⅓ of egg whites with chocolate mixture. Carefully fold in remaining egg whites. Pour into ungreased 2-quart casserole. Bake 50 to 60 minutes or until table knife inserted 2 inches from edge comes out clean.

Serves 6.

MOTHER DOWD'S

Lemon Cream Freeze

2 eggs	2 cups milk
½ cup sugar	¼ cup lemon juice
½ cup light corn syrup	1 tsp. grated lemon rind

Beat eggs until foamy throughout. Add sugar gradually and beat until thick and lemon colored. Add remaining ingredients and mix until well combined. Divide in half in 2 freezer trays and freeze 2 to 3 hours or until almost frozen. Remove from freezer trays and whip until light and creamy. Return to freezer and freeze until firm. Serves 6.

MOTHER DOWD'S

Chocolate Cheese Frosting

3 ozs. soft cream cheese	2 cups sifted powdered
1 Tb. milk	sugar
1 square unsweetened	1 tsp. vanilla
chocolate, melted	¼ tsp. salt

Blend cream cheese, milk and chocolate. Gradually add sugar, beating well after each addition. Add vanilla and salt. Continue beating until light and fluffy.

Makes 1 cup.

Index